MW01383245

"Maria Olsen's new book is a timely and illuminating reminder that the American family now appears in many different forms. She uses engaging first-hand accounts to tell the stories of parents who have taken a non-traditional path to creating their family—from adoption, to opting not to have children, to single-parenting to choosing a partner of a different race or of the same sex. Their stories are compelling to read and help us widen our definition of family to include all paradigms."

—Clare Cushman, U.S. Supreme Court Historian and author of *Court watchers: Eyewitness Accounts in Supreme Court History*

"Maria Olsen understands more than most people the impact of our changing country that is no longer a map of Cleavers. The author is mixed race and singleminded in her mission to educate and empower a new America that is a mosaic of colors and cultures—and levels of acceptance."

—Iris Krasnow, bestselling author of *Surrendering to Marriage* and *I Am My Mother's Daughter* and journalism/women's studies professor at American University

"Families are changing, and Maria Olsen's book, and her life experience, offer the perfect guide to help us understand our new world. It's a must-read for all parents who are trying to raise children in our diverse family culture while making sense of it ourselves."

—Kimberly Palmer, Senior Money Editor of U.S. News & World Report and author of *Smart Mom, Rich Mom*

"*Not the Cleaver Family* is a brilliant and much needed commentary on family in modern culture. Maria Olsen helps us to redefine what 'normal' means, and to accept ourselves just as we are. A must-read for anyone interested in human relations and life in general!"

—Dr. Anita Gadhia-Smith, Psychotherapist and author of *How To Stay Together: Whether You Want To or Not*

"Maria Olsen has written a lucid, sensitive book that advances our understanding of the many types of marriages we see around us. Deeply researched, using real-life stories and statistics, this book expands our idea of marriage, and will help build the cultural inclusion these unions deserve."

—Robin Gerber, author of *Leadership the Eleanor Roosevelt Way*

NOT THE CLEAVER FAMILY

THE NEW NORMAL IN MODERN AMERICAN FAMILIES

NOT THE CLEAVER FAMILY

With light & gratitude —

MARIA LEONARD OLSEN

Maria Leonard Olsen

TATE PUBLISHING
AND ENTERPRISES, LLC

Published by Tate Publishing & Enterprises, LLC
127 E. Trade Center Terrace | Mustang, Oklahoma 73064 USA
1.888.361.9473 | www.tatepublishing.com

Tate Publishing is committed to excellence in the publishing industry. The company reflects the philosophy established by the founders, based on Psalm 68:11,
"The Lord gave the word and great was the company of those who published it."

Book design copyright © 2016 by Tate Publishing, LLC. All rights reserved.
Cover design by Joana Quilantang
Interior design by Gram Telen

Published in the United States of America
ISBN: 978-1-68319-039-4
Family & Relationships / Alternative Family
16.09.01

To Caroline

and Christopher—

I am honored to be your mother

Acknowledgments

I spoke to hundreds of people across the country about their families and experiences. Some pseudonyms are used, as well as only first names, in cases where people asked to remain anonymous. I am honored by those who shared their stories of pain, growth, and acceptance, and I am grateful to all who agreed to speak to me about their unique—and normal—American family.

Contents

Preface:

This Is My Family

In 2013, the US Census Bureau reported that within a year, white children under the age of five will be a minority and that by 2043, less than 50 percent of the US population will be white.[1] The typical American family no longer resembles the lily-white Cleavers[2] of a generation ago.

While Americans are learning to embrace diversity, discrimination and ignorance still abound. Recent events in Ferguson, Missouri, are a painful and stark reminder. Unfortunately, it is not apocryphal that President Obama was mistaken for a waiter at a black-tie function, as I have been as a brown-skinned woman by an elderly white woman at a prestigious country club in the Washington, D.C., metropolitan area. Or that recent commercials featuring mixed race or same-sex parents were launched

---

1   http://www.census.gov/prod/cen2010/briefs/c2010br-14.pdf

2   A popular television show during the 1950s and 1960s *Leave it to Beaver* featured a wholesome white family in which Ward Cleaver was the wise, calm father, the mother June Cleaver always wore a dress and pearls, and the two children learned an important life lesson by the end of each episode.

by blue chip companies and were met with both applause and criticism.

When I was growing up in a suburb of Washington, D.C., I was the only dark-skinned person in my school. People made jokes about me that stung.

I was also the only person in my grade from a "broken home," a term not used so much anymore, now that approximately 50 percent of American marriages end in divorce. There were some girls in my Kensington, Maryland, parochial school who were forbidden from playing with me because my parents were divorced—and therefore excommunicated from the Catholic church—in the 1970s. Women lacked significant power and my non-citizen mother feared deportation after her divorce from my American father.

Flash forward four decades to a successful legal career and a political appointment. I have two beautiful children for whom I was frequently mistaken to be their nanny—even by other neighborhood nannies. I wrote a children's book, *Mommy, Why's Your Skin So Brown?*,[3] as a way of talking to my own children about why so many people mistook their darker-skinned mother for their babysitter and to share with other children how people often let their curiosity overwhelm their manners.

When my parents married in 1961, it was illegal for them to do so in the state of Maryland, a state considered by most to be liberal. Interracial marriage was illegal in sixteen states until the UnitedStates Supreme Court nullified such state laws in 1967.[4] My parents had to go to the District of Columbia, a few miles away, to tie the knot. Most people I know are very surprised when I tell them that.

---

3   Mirror Publishing 2013. See https://www.facebook.com/MommyWhysYourSkinSoBrown; www.mariaolsen49.wix.com/author

4   *Loving v. Virginia*, 388 U.S. 1 (1967)

A generation from now, the children of my children will be surprised to hear analogous stories about same-sex unions. But that will be the case. While I was writing this book, the US Supreme Court struck down laws banning same-sex marriage. In my circle of friends and family, my sister-in-law legally married her female partner. My close friend parented a daughter without a partner. Other friends adopted or chose to have one or no children at all. Though my grandparents-in-law-to-be asked, upon seeing my photo, if I could speak English, I married their white grandson, who was raised in a religion different than mine. Our landscape of families continues to evolve.

Today's media reflects the changes. The Emmy Award-winning television show *Modern Family* premiered in 1989 and continues to be watched by more than twelve million viewers each week. It features a gay couple with an adopted child, a mixed race couple, a blended family, and an older man with a younger wife.[5]

This book examines the contemporary American family. It is based on hundreds of interviews with families across the country about intimate and public details of their lives and illustrates how the normative paradigm of the family has changed in this country. Same-sex marriages are not uncommon. Single women are having babies without partners to help them. More couples are childless by choice.

---

5   http://abc.go.com/shows/modern-family

From stories collected across the country, empirically sound generalizations may be made about the scope of change and about the lingering ignorance fueling negative reactions to such changes. It is a consciousness-raising effort to help educators and citizens who hope to remain aware of—and appreciate—our changing society. It is also a reflection with relief and gratitude that my children are coming of age in a generation largely unencumbered by the judgments, assumptions and expectations that had deleterious effects on my self-perception at critical junctures in my life. It took me almost until I reached fifty years of age to feel comfortable about my complicated, colorful, mixed family. My mixed-race children do not have to choose as I did between race boxes on various forms that don't fit them. My gay son some day can legally marry a man that he loves, unlike the many closeted homosexuals I knew when I was growing up. Our nation is embracing the changing nature of our families, and that is something to celebrate.

The author, her children, and her former husband

Childfree by Choice

"I feel my life is full without children."

—Devon McLaughlin, of
York, Pennsylvania

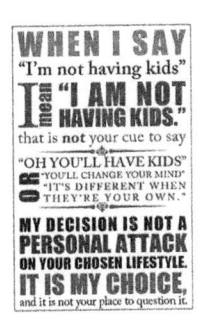

WHEN I SAY "I'm not having kids" I mean "I AM NOT HAVING KIDS." that is **not** your cue to say "OH YOU'LL HAVE KIDS" "YOU'LL CHANGE YOUR MIND" "IT'S DIFFERENT WHEN THEY'RE YOUR OWN." MY DECISION IS NOT A PERSONAL ATTACK ON YOUR CHOSEN LIFESTYLE. IT IS MY CHOICE, and it is not your place to question it.

Having been raised by strong women heavily influenced by their Filipina cultural norms, I was expected to be a doctor or a lawyer *and* to have children. Exactly nine months after marrying, my grandmother began questioning me about whether I was yet pregnant. I have a strong maternal instinct and love being a mother to my two children. I am fortunate that I was able to chapter my life and reenter the legal field after my children left for school.

As I progressed in the legal field, I noticed that many of the most successful female lawyers had no children. But our culture at large seemed to equate "womanhood" with "motherhood." The stereotypical successful businesswoman displayed "male" attributes of being tough, driven, and oftentimes ruthless. Digging deeper, however, I discovered many women led self-fulfilled lives while choosing to remain childfree.

Perhaps the greatest gift of the feminist movement is women's ability to choose their paths among many more options. Whether or not to have children is, for many today, a choice. And the choice not to have children is increasingly common today. The Pew Research Center reported last year that the United States has one of the highest rates of childlessness in the world.[1] The US birth rate also has fallen to a record low.[2]

Many men and women I interviewed cited the desire not to bring children into a violent world, the environmental impact of overpopulation, negative childhood experiences, career concerns, financial issues, and the lack of maternal/ paternal instinct as the reasons for their decision not to

---

1   http://www.pewresearch.org/fact-tank/2014/01/03/in-terms-of-childlessness-u-s-ranks-near-the-top-worldwide/

2   http://www.pewsocialtrends.org/2012/11/29/u-s-birth-rate-falls-to-a-record-low-decline-is-greatest-among-immigrants/

procreate. Alan, of Los Angeles, and his partner like their lives without having to care for children. Laura, of Chevy Chase, Maryland, cited her husband's fear of parenting as the reason she probably will never have children. Sarah, a Bethesda, Maryland, elementary school teacher, spends "enough" time with children during her teaching hours. Paulette, a former school principal in College Park, Maryland, and her partner of forty years, Eileen, never married and never felt the desire to have children, with the hundreds of children in their professional lives. Anne Armstrong, a museum curator, attorney, and former Air Force captain, of Washington, D.C., harbors no maternal instinct, and had a husband who never wanted children and a varied career that left little time for kids. Mike and his partner in New York City summed their decision up with the simple observation that they were "just too selfish" to bring children into their already busy lives. Every one of these interviewees was aware of the kid-centric culture's bias towards having children, however, and battled negative comments and insinuations based on their own paths. All had strangers who had tried to made them feel that they failed to live life completely in some way.

Feminist writer Katie Roiphe wrote: "Childlessness may be one of the last vibrant taboos in our culture. Women, especially, who don't have children are still regarded as somehow incomplete or thwarted, even by liberal and tolerant people. It may be that childless women are viewed, covertly, in some quarters, as selfish or unnatural or unfeminine. But the most common reaction now is pity—the idea that these women are missing out on one of life's greatest experiences."[3]

Times may be changing for this subset of our population, however. The *TIME* magazine cover of August 12, 2013, exalted "The Childfree Life: When Having It All Means Not Having Children." The cover story author noted that the American birth rate is at a record low. "The idea that women don't have babies because they are 'selfish' is not only reductive, in so many cases, it is simply incorrect," posits the then-forty-one-year-old writer.[4]

Newsweek,[5] CBS News,[6] and many other major news outlets have featured stories on the childless. The *Huffington Post* has a Childfree section for readers and contributors.[7]

---

3   *The Washington Post*, April 5, 2015.

4   Sandler, Lauren. "The Childfree Life: When Having It All Means Not Having Children" *TIME*, August 12, 2013.

5   http://www.newsweek.com/childless-and-proud-it-195054; http://www.newsweek.com/does-having-children-make-you-happy-91157.

6   http://www.cbsnews.com/videos/childless-couples-who-choose-not-to-have-children/

7   http://www.huffingtonpost.com/news/childfree

Popular media is recognizing the steady rise of this demographic. And the emphasis is changing from those who cannot have children to those who choose not to do so.

© Phil Date

The cultural imperative to have children is aptly described in numerous recent books, such as *The Childless Revolution*,[8] describing the childfree as "the fastest-growing demographic group to emerge in decades"; *Complete Without Kids: An Insider's Guide to Childfree Living by Choice or by Chance*,[9] a psychologist's description of the unique issues that childfree adults face simply due to living in a culture that celebrates babies and traditional families;

---

8 Madelyn Cain, *The Childless Revolution: What It Means To Be Childless Today* (Da Capo Press, 2001).

9 Ellen Walker, *Complete Without Kids: An Insider's Guide to Childfree Living by Choice or by Chance* (Greenleaf Book Group, 2011).

Reconceiving Women: Separating Motherhood from Female Identity,[10] reframes childlessness as a concept and lays a groundwork for an expanded view of women's identity and psychic development; *Pride And Joy: The Lives And Passions Of Women Without Children*,[11] stories dispelling the social myth that women must have children to be happy, and debunking the stereotypes of childless women; *Otherhood: Modern Women Finding A New Kind of Happiness*,[12] memoir and postfeminist battle cry on behalf of childless women; *Childfree and Loving It!*,[13] a journalist's investigation into the reasons women choose to be childfree and the social stigma surrounding that choice; *Selfish, Shallow, and Self-Absorbed: Sixteen Writers on the Decision Not to Have Kids*,[14] acclaimed female writers explain why they have chosen to eschew motherhood; *Kidfree & Lovin' It!–Whether by Choice, Chance or Circumstance: The complete guide to living*

---

10 Mardy Ireland, PhD, *Reconceiving Women: Separating Motherhood from Female Identity* (Guilford Press 1993).

11 Terri Casey, *Pride And Joy: The Lives And Passions Of Women Without Children* (Atria Books, 2007).

12 Melanie Notkin, *Otherhood: Modern Women Finding A New Kind of Happiness* (Seal Press, 2014).

13 Nicki Defago, *Childfree and Loving It!* (Vision, 2005).

14 Meghan Daum, *Selfish, Shallow, and Self-Absorbed: Sixteen Writers on the Decision Not to Have Kids* (Picador, 2015).

as a non-parent,[15] a survey of more than four thousand nonparents on why they chose not to parent and the issues they face for not doing so; and *Two Is Enough: A Couple's Guide to Living Childless by Choice*,[16] exploring the growing childlessness trend, to name a few.

Laura Scott, the Florida-based author of *Two is Enough: A Couple's Guide to Living Childless by Choice*, founded the Childless by Choice Project.[17] Her Childless by Choice Project website serves as a much-used reference and marketing tool for journalists, project participants, researchers, and the general public. The author and life coach has a Childless by Choice film project in the development and early production stage.

---

15 Kaye Walters, *Kidfree & Lovin' It!–Whether by Choice, Chance or Circumstance: The complete guide to living as a non-parent* (Serena Bay Publishing, 2012).

16 Laura Scott, *Two Is Enough: A Couple's Guide to Living Childless by Choice* (Seal Press, 2009).

17 www.childlessbychoiceproject.com

Author, Laura Scott, of Tampa, Florida

Scott, childfree at age fifty-three, describes her experience:

> Like many of the decisions we make in life, my decision to remain childless was motivated in part by fear—fear of regret. I was afraid to take the risk that I might be a bitter, unhappy, or regretful mom. Given my disinterest in the role of parent, this was a real possibility—particularly when I started hearing from parents who felt compelled to speak out, saying things like "You're lucky not to have kids. They will break your heart." In my mid-thirties, as I became increasingly comfortable identifying myself as childless by choice, I started hearing comments like these from parents who felt equally comfortable in the presence of a childfree person to share some of their personal turmoil about parenthood. At first I was shocked, since some of the people who were sharing with me were women and men I knew who had raised "good" children, who were seemingly happy and capable parents. Soon, I became accustomed to

being pulled into corners, lowered voices imploring, "Please don't share this with anyone...." I came away from those hushed confessions feeling like I was privy to the best-kept secret in the world: A surprising number of outwardly happy parents have misgivings or regrets about parenthood. At first I felt justified in my choice to remain childless, but mostly I felt sad, especially for those men and women who told me they'd never imagined they had the choice not to be a parent. I was left to wonder if these feelings came from their difficult experiences as parents, or if they were regretful because they didn't feel they'd had a choice in the matter. On the other side of the spectrum, I had many encounters with parents who endorsed parenthood enthusiastically, usually in response to my confession that I was devoid of any maternal feelings. They told me I would change my mind, that "it's different when they're yours." They credited their children with bringing joy and wonder to their lives, and they seemed frustrated or sad about my childfree status because clearly, I didn't get it. I was "missing out" on a whole dimension of experience, the lack of which would leave me less than whole. Being alternately envied and pitied was bewildering for me. So was the realization that some people believed I had remained childless because I was selfish, immature, lazy, materialistic, or a kid hater—none of which was good, all of which was at odds with how I perceived myself. This disparity between how I was perceived and how I actually felt forced me to question my own ideas about myself and my life. Was I a freak? A slacker? Was I developmentally disabled—in some kind of arrested state, like Peter Pan? Did I have an obligation to procreate? The assumptions people often make about the voluntarily childless troubled me because they didn't come close to capturing my complex motives. I was not motivated to remain childless because I didn't like kids or because I wanted to spend my money on cars and diamonds instead of cribs and diapers. I was motivated to be childfree because there was so much about my life that I enjoyed and so much that I still wanted to do, experiences that I felt I would have to delay or forgo if I had children. I remained childless because I valued my freedom to do the things I thought I could do well and happily, things I had dreamed of doing all my life. The fact that parenthood was conspicuously absent from my "ten things to do before I die" list spoke volumes. I had no desire, no longing, to have a child to call my own. Rocking a child to sleep or breastfeeding an infant held no appeal for me, and on the few occasions when I did hold an infant in my arms, I felt awkward and inept. I had decided that Mom was not a role I was well suited for, much the same way I'd determined I would never be a mathematician or a veterinarian.[18]

---

18 From *Two is Enough: A Couple's Guide to Living Childless by Choice*, by Laura Scott, copyright © 2009. Reprinted by permission of Seal Press, a member of The Perseus Books Group.

In 2015, a collection of prominent authors' essays was published in *Selfish, Shallow, and Self-Absorbed—Sixteen Writers on the Decision Not to Have Kids*. In reviewing the book, Katie Roiphe noted:

> It is possible to rethink the subtle, implicit judgments against the childless, the attitudes of pity or condescension or secret belief that they are missing out, the oppressive conversion fantasy itself; one can envy their lightness, their unspooling hours of day-dreamy thought, their unfettered relationships with other people's children, their last minute plane tickets, their wandering midnight conversations with friends after dinner, their weeks of single-minded devotion to work. One can appreciate a truly alternative life, without prejudice.... The idea that some women and men prefer not to have children is often met with sharp criticism and incredulity by the public and mainstream media. In this provocative and controversial collection of essays, curated by writer Meghan Daum, thirteen acclaimed female writers explain why they have chosen to eschew motherhood. Contributors include Lionel Shriver, Sigrid Nunez, Kate Christensen, Elliott Holt, Geoff Dyer, and Tim Kreider, among others, who will give a unique perspective on the overwhelming cultural pressure of parenthood.[19]

---

19 *The Washington Post*, April 5, 2015.

The Internet is replete with childfree blogs, Web sites, and social media pages supporting those who choose not to have children. A few examples include www.thechildfreelife.com,[20] which books itself as a safe haven in a baby-crazed world"; Cheerfully Childfree,[21] a "sanctuary to consider, become, and remain Childfree without the backlash of breeders who can't accept us for who we choose to be;" https://www.reddit.com/r/childfree/, an online childfree community that, among other things, catalogs media pro, con and neutral on the subject and; http://thenotmom.com/, spotlighting the unique perspectives and legacies of women childless, "by choice or by chance," and host of a "NotMom Summit."

There is an International Childfree Day, begun in 2013 as an annual recognition of childfree people and their lives, and as a way to foster the acceptance of the childfree choice in today's society. It built upon a 1973 "Non-Parents Day" event in New York City that was celebrated by the National

20 TheChildfreeLife.com, is "a friendly and supportive environment for people who don't intend to have kids, as well as those who are still undecided about becoming a parent." Their Facebook page provides links to recent articles and conversations on their site, keeping readers up to date on the latest Childfree Life activities. Their Zazzle page sells greeting cards geared towards those who choose not to have children. http://www.zazzle.com/thechildfreelife.

21 https://www.facebook.com/CheerfullyChildfree

Alliance for Optional Parenthood. Support for the event continues to build.

The process of arriving at the decision to remain childless of course varied from person to person. For example, Kristina Krawchuk, of Ashburn, Virginia, knew from the time she was in high school that she did not want to have children. And her high-powered broadcasting career did not lend itself to raising kids. She didn't feel the maternal pull and certainly doesn't feel that she missed anything that was needed in her life. She feels no need to be apologetic about her choice and had no pressure from her extended family to procreate. She made her mind up early about children and never looked back.

Similarly, Rockville, Maryland, couple Kate and David revel in their lives as "perpetual DINKS" (that is, Double Income, No Kids). They enjoy their freedom, and while they like other people's children, they don't feel the need to have children of their own. While they are both still young, they doubt they will change their mind about remaining childfree.

Linda, a former World Bank economist, and her commercial land developer husband decided their lives were full without children. Linda traveled out of the country at least six months every year, and her husband was scarcely home due to his business demands. The Boyds, Maryland, couple deliberated over the decision when Linda entered her early forties. The couple decided not to have children. Linda says she "fulfills her maternal desires caring for [her] four horses and four dogs, as well as doting on her nieces from time to time." Linda feels no regret about their decision but notes that some people believe it to be "selfish."

Many high-powered couples put their careers first—a common choice—then have the childbearing decision made for them, in a sense. While couples who wait beyond a woman's fertility period limit their options, many do choose adoption. Or by not making a decision, a decision is made for them, by nature or circumstance.

Scott Sonntag and Mary Lynn Reed of Washington, D.C., both have active, high-pressured legal careers. They married relatively late, by American standards, and found that having children simply never happened for them. While each loves children, and Scott has three adult children from a previous marriage who the couple considers their kids, they explored adoption but decided against it and are comfortable with their decision. And their three golden retrievers are incredibly spoiled!

Cyndy Esty, a Chevy Chase, Maryland high tech consultant, like many others with whom I spoke, kept waiting for the right time to have children, "with stability in relationship and finance, and the combination never worked out when cancer came into the mix…Very different from my life plan as a child thinking I would get a degree.

Work. Marry. Have two kids and have grandchildren. I got all that through being a stepmom. Who knew? Life doesn't always turn out according to the diary of our childhood. But it is better than what I could ever imagine and I could never have planned this. I am now achieving my dreams and enjoying being a loving Nona to my stepgrandbaby. Like the movie *Under the Tuscan Sun*—you might get what you wished for, but not the way and in the order you thought."

Married Tucson, Arizona, resident Lisa reflected: "In my thirties, I could not imagine that I would ever be happy without children. Now in my fifties, I appreciate the wonderful life I've had and hope to continue to have. Children turned out not to be the key to my happiness. Having come from a traditional family with a mom, dad and kids, I never thought of families with only two..., but that's what I have and I still feel blessed!"

Of course whether or not to have children is perhaps the most personal choice one can make. While raising children is rife with challenges, it is a choice I have never regretted. I chuckle to myself, however, recalling the time I heard four mothers in a row complain about the problems they were having with their teen and adult children during a twelve-step recovery meeting several months ago. When it became the fifth woman's time to share, she simply stated, "I'm just glad I never had children."

People, especially women, who have made the choice to remain childfree still overwhelmingly feel judged for their choice. But the tide has shifted considerably and continues to do so.

Mixed-Race Families

"What are you?"

—asked countless times of
Matthew Tucker,
Kensington, Maryland

© Rawpixelimages

Our society has come a long way from the sentiments expressed in the groundbreaking 1967 film *Guess Who's Coming to Dinner?* in which white parents are shocked at the black boyfriend their daughter brought home for dinner. Currently, the world's best golfer, Tiger Woods, is biracial and married a white woman. White supermodel Heidi Klum married the black musician, Seal. The First Lady on the prime time television show *Scandal* is

African-American and married to a white president. The president depicted on the popular television show *24* is black. Our actual president is a product of a mixed-race marriage (although our category-obsessed society more commonly refers to him as black). Reality television star Kim Kardashian is in a mixed-race marriage with one of America's best known rappers, Kanye West. Actor Will Smith's latest leading lady is white. Republican presidential candidate Jeb Bush is married to a Latina woman, and together, they have bilingual and bicultural children. Billboards and Web sites often feature mixed-race couples. Ads from major American companies like Ford, Pillsbury and Swiffer use multiracial families to sell their wares. Mixed has gone mainstream.

But discomfort with differences still lingers. The best-selling Cheerios brand cereal caused a splash when the family featured on its much-aired commercial consisted of a black father, a white mother, and a mixed-race daughter. A website, "We are the 15 percent," with photos of mixed-race families across the country was started in response to the backlash from the commercial's airing.[1] "We've created this site to publicly reflect the changing face of the American

---

1 We Are the 15 Percent is a crowd-sourced website collection of portraits of American interracial families and marriages, inspired by the Cheerios ad. The title refers to the statistic that 14.6 percent of new marriages in America are interracial, according to the 2008 Census. www.wearethe15percent.com

family. According to the 2008 census, 15% of new marriages are interracial. And yet, it still feels rare to see something like the Cheerios ad represented in mainstream culture."

The Watkins/White family of Washington, D.C.

I still don't want my mixed-race children going to college or living in the South. When my mother came to the United States in the early 60s, Washington, D.C.'s ubiquitous "no colored" signs sometimes applied to her and sometimes did not (In her experience, brown skin was less objectionable, or at least noticed, than black). She influenced my perception that it was safer for dark-skinned people to remain in the northeastern United States.

Almost every biracial or multiracial person I have met has been irked by the "What are you?" or "Where are you from?" questions.[2] I face these seemingly every day. Because of my appearance, people speak to me in Spanish at least once a week, even though my dark skin comes from my Pacific Islander mother and not Latin America, as so many assume. But the questions present a forced choice for many biracial people--whether they identify more with one facet of their ancestry or are compelled to choose, based on their appearance.

Professor Jinah Kim, the assistant director of the Asian American Studies Program at Northwestern University in Evanston, Illinois, writes about comparative race and the racial diaspora in the United States. She currently lives in metropolitan Chicago but spent different parts of her life living on both coasts.

"Being Asian is so different in California versus New York," Kim says. "Asians have been in California for many more generations."

Kim notices that the mixed-race students at North-western University are a powerful constituency at the school and have an opportunity to shape what's happen-

---

2   There are some hilarious YouTube videos satirizing scenarios in which such questions are asked. See, for example, "What Kind of Asian Are You?" by helpmefindparents, www.youtube. com/watch?v=DWynJkN5HbQ; and "If Asians Said The Stuff White People Say," by BuzzFeed, www.youtube.com/watch?v= PMJI1Dw83Hc&index=5&list=RDDWynJkN5HbQ

ing in the university's culture. "While it's still difficult and complicated to be mixed, there's a certain kind of traction here. But racism is not over. There still are the common questions of 'who are you' and 'what are you?'"

As on other college campuses, Northwestern has groups for black students, Asian students, Jewish students, Catholic students, and others. Unlike in my college days, however, there is a group for students of mixed cultural heritage. "MIXED (the Mixed Race Student Coalition) was founded in 2013 to provide a space for those who identify with a mixed race background or have interest in mixed race affairs/cross cultural collaboration through social and academic events, discussion, and support." My daughter is an active member. She describes it as "what one wants it to be; we all have different mixed experiences. If you want it to be a place where you don't feel different [being of mixed ancestry], it can be. If it's a space where you want your experience of difference validated, it can also be that."

Marlene Lenthang, a Northwestern student, describes her experience and that of her classmates so eloquently in a presentation she made at MIXED:

> Growing up in Chicago with an Ecuadorian mother and Indian father, I felt like a wandering soul. My sister and I seemed to be the only humans in the

world to wander in this crevice between these two very different countries with two very different cultures.

Ever since I was a kid, I've struggled with being categorized. Or rather, other people struggled. Elementary school teachers would mark me down as the wrong race, strangers would play the guessing game with my ethnicity, and the racial check boxes of standardized tests never seemed to apply to me. Because the teachers, strangers, and the rest of the world seemed confused about whom I was, I became confused too. I didn't feel Indian like the Indian girls in my classes that wore pretty saris. I didn't feel Hispanic, as all Mexican people from my neighborhood were. Soon, after hearing it enough, I adopted my mom's go-to line, "She is half Indian, half Ecuadorian," and I adopted it with pride. I didn't want to be mistaken for anything else anymore. I didn't want the coos of "how exotic" or "what a mix!" I just wanted to be me.

But in a world obsessed with categories and labels, it isn't so easy. This is the mixed race experience: the ups and downs of being of a multiracial background and a racially ambiguous appearance. This experience belongs to the fastest growing population in the United States. In fact, according to the Pew Research Center, the mixed race population is growing faster than the nation as a whole.

When Sara Hou was younger she used to sit next to her white mother at family gatherings round a large wooden dining table. The table was stuffed with food and surrounded by her father's Chinese family. The family would talk and jest in Chinese, the incomprehensible tongue playing liking music to her ears, broken by the frequent eruption of laughter. Her father, wiping away tears, would look to his daughter and wife, translating, "Oh! This is what he said…" Sara, with her porcelain skin and upward slanting eyes, acknowledged the translated joke in feeble, polite laughter. But it wasn't quite the same.

Nick Davis was on the trolley up to the Getty Museum in Los Angeles with his white mother and black father. He was a giddy seven-year-old pointing to the window view of the Los Angeles skyline, practicing his newly learned word *tacky*. "Hey, Mom, look there! You know that's tacky!" His mother nodded softly. "That's right, honey." A white woman smiled and approached little Nick, asking his mother, "What is the father? Is he Mexican?" Nick's mother blinked in shock. She thought the question *What is the father?* didn't even make grammatical sense and her husband was standing right beside her. The woman continued, "Is your child Mexican?" Angered, Nick's mother replied in a huff, "No, my child is mine and my husband's," gesturing to her husband. The woman's surprised eyes darted from Nick to his mother to his father. "It's none of your business what race my child is. He is my child, he is not Mexican." The woman, offended, walked away saying, "I was just asking." From that moment, Nick felt like all eyes were on him. He was racially ambiguous. People did not know how to pin him, but they kept trying.

Family is everything in the Abel household. On Sunday summer days, Jennifer's Filipino cousins and Honduran and Mexican cousins come together for a garage barbeque in the Chicago heat. Sitting at the table in between two different cultures, Jennifer often felt victimized, at odds with the people around her, at odds with herself. She looked different with light skin that mismatched everyone else's complexion, honey-colored curls, eyes that slightly slant at the end and lips that purse in confidence. "Oh Jennifer, your nose is flat, you must get that from your father's side," Hispanic cousins would say. "Jennifer, you're so dark, you don't look as white as your mom," Filipino aunties would point out. Each side of her family continued noting the differences in her, shredding her cultural halves to bits. She is proud to be of two distinct cultures and to have a family that comes together, but hates to bear the comments of microaggression and cultural racist complexes. Family is everything, but why can't they let her be?

The mixed race population has existed for centuries in the United States, dating back to the first colonizers.

Next year will mark the 50-year anniversary of the US Supreme Court case of *Loving v. Virginia*, which ended laws prohibiting interracial marriage. Just sixteen years ago the US Census Bureau gave Americans the option to check multiple race boxes to define themselves. And just eight years ago, the United States elected a biracial president, Barack Obama. All of these are factors in explaining the growing number of multiracial individuals.

The 2010 US Census approximated 2.1 percent of the population as multiracial, which comes out to 9 million individuals. Last year that percentage jumped to 6.9 percent. The Pew Research Center says that the actual number of mixed-race Americans is nearly triple what the Census counts.

If the mixed race population is so large and growing, why aren't we talking about it? The mixed race conversation exists; it just depends where you are. States with a strong history of immigration and colonial history have more multiracial discourse.

Northwestern University Professor Nitasha Sharma reflects upon the importance of geography in her home state Hawaii, where the mixed race group makes up 23 percent of the population.

"To me this [mixed race] conversation is not really happening on the West Coast or in Hawaii because it's already a part of the dominant conversation and reality," explains Professor Sharma, who will teach a class next quarter entitled The Mixed Race Experience. "But in other places, it's harder. In places where people really identify with just one race in a highly segregated city like Chicago, how does the multiracial traverse or even find community when the ideas of people are so separate?"

It's no coincidence that these spaces and discourses of mixed race people have burgeoned on college campuses. The movement of student mixed race groups began in the 1990s, inspired by the Hapa movement, the movement of explaining multiracial identity (Gordon, 2013). *Hapa* is a word that comes from Hawaii and refers to people of mixed ethnic heritage, but was adopted on California campuses to create clubs for students of half-Asian heritage. The Hapa movement became a springboard for creating clubs for multiracial students of all backgrounds, not just Asian.

Today, schools stretching the California coast like UCLA and UC Davis to the Ivy League coast at Brown University and Columbia University have spaces for students of multiple races, most emerging in the past decade. Not only are clubs emerging, but universities are holding and supporting conferences dedicated to the professional study and research of mixed race. UC Berkeley holds an annual conference dedicated to the subject with themes such as the language revolving with mixed race. DePaul University in Chicago has also hosted three Critical Mixed Race Conferences, the first of which in 2010 had more than four hundred attendees.

"There was this energy in the room, people just really felt that they were hungry for this space. We realized there's a whole cohort of young people who want information on these topics. They think, I really want to do this work but it's not validated by an academy," says conference founder Professor Laura Kina. "We're not trying to save the world, we're just trying to legitimize the work people have already been doing."

Northwestern University's MIXED club itself is a case study of the hunger for support, community, and academia on multiracial topics. The group has hosted bone marrow drives, interracial dating panels and is currently planning their own Mixed Race Studies conference to be held on campus in fall 2017.

Davis is the President of MIXED, a club that started just two years ago. In today's meeting, members write a question on a slip of paper, fold it, mix the folded notes and pick one at random to share. "Does being mixed affect your dating patterns?" "Do you think your siblings have a different mixed experience than you?" Students speak up freely, no need for raised hands or polite filters. This is their space. "I think for a lot of nonblack guys, I'm considered the "approachable" black girl," "We call my brother the closeted Asian

because he doesn't embrace his Filipino side at all."
"My brother looks more Hispanic so he could fit into
that group; I on the other hand was never accepted
by campus Latinas." Free flowing streams of thought,
laughs, and nods of agreement ripple within the room.
It's fascinating that all these students find common
ground in these experiences, but they couldn't be a more
different looking bunch. Blond curls next to electric
blue braids, an afro next to a sheet of shiny black hair.
Despite the physical differences, their experiences
resonate a chord much deeper than the physical. These
students needed this space, where they could freely
talk about how they've felt misunderstood. A place
to express the pain of microaggressions, the everyday
comments that intentionally or unintentionally harbor
racism. A place to answer society's bugging question
of "what are you?" for themselves. A place to explore
one's identity.

"When I came to college MIXED felt like the
most comfortable place for me because even though
my mixed identity was important to me, I didn't
really know if I would fit in with Kaibigan [the
Northwestern University club for Filipino students]
and the people who I perceived to be more truly
Filipino," explains MIXED member Caroline Olsen.
"MIXED has helped me understand that I can be
100 percent MIXED and also 100 percent Danish
and 100 percent Filipino. They're not fractions of me,
they're all full, valid parts of my identity."

To the lofty hands that wave away mixed race as insignificant, to the eyes that cannot see mixed race as an important issue, I'll lay it plainly: Mixed race people have often felt different and out of place all their lives. Creating a space for themselves is creating a place of rest. It is creating community where they can find people like them and an end to placing themselves in boxes where they did not fit. A place to embrace who they are and find validity in being their unique selves.

I have spent my entire adolescence in question of where I belonged. I constantly placed myself beside the people I thought I could conform the most to, but never found a true sense of community. I never felt white, black, Asian or Hispanic enough. MIXED was the first time I encountered a space where not only was it okay to be uncategorizable, it was celebrated and validated.

"Coming into college, I wasn't sure what it would mean to be a black student at the university," says Nick who is white, black and American Indian. "I knew what it meant to be black in my neighborhood and I had to work to do that. I didn't want to start over validating myself for another unknown black community."

The generation before mine created many support groups for multiracial families in an unaccepting society. Today's birthed a place of support for those children, and is working toward creating a more open and accepting society for tomorrow.

"I hope that by the time my kid ends up in elementary school, they wont need to accept what their peers consider them to be," expresses Sara. "They will be the voice that says hey, I'm this, this and this. I can't be placed and checked into one box."

After I finished speaking, my friends nearby pulled me into a hug. I felt like I had just revealed myself naked in front of my peers. I had never explained to anyone how I hated being pinned as the wrong ethnicity, my childhood frustration, the microaggressions I encountered in college, my feelings. I haven't even told my parents. I felt shaky, proud, and for once completely released and relieved. No longer would I have to harbor these little burdens, I found a place that understands. And as the statistics increasingly point out that the future of the United States will be the mixed race face, I could not be more proud. Perhaps it'll be a face like mine, uncategorizable, indefinable, 100 percent mixed.

I wish there had been such an organization at my college when I was there. I always felt like an outsider. We learn to categorize from an early age in this country. I didn't look white, and when I went to the Philippines, I sounded very American. I would have liked a place to meet others like me.

Best-selling author Heidi Durrow has made numerous efforts to bridge the divide for people like me. She hosts an audio and video podcast, "The Mixed Experience," and was an original host and producer of Mixed Chicks Chat, the award-winning weekly podcast that ran from 2007 to 2012. Through interviews, essays, reviews, and ruminations, Durrow talks about the varying aspects of the mixed experience in the arts, culture, academia, and history. As the daughter of an African American father and a Danish mother, she calls herself an "Afro-Viking" and "a mixed chick trying to make sense of a mixed-up world." Durrow also started the annual Mixed Remixed Festival in Los Angeles.[3] In 2014, more than seven hundred multiracial and multicultural families and individuals enjoyed the day of workshops, panel presentations, film screenings, readings,

---

3   "The *Mixed Remixed Festival* is the nation's premiere cultural arts festival celebrating stories of the Mixed experience, multiracial and multicultural families and individuals through films, books and performance. The *Festival* brings together film and book lovers, innovative and emerging artists, and multiracial families and individuals, Hapas, and families of transracial adoption for workshops, readings, film screenings and live performance including music, comedy, and spoken word.... [Their] goal is to dismantle racism and prejudice and foster communication and connectedness in a unique way—through storytelling." www.mixedremixed.org

and performances. The festival grows every year, and in 2016 I was on a panel discussing multiracial children's literature and excavating family mythology.

The Mixed Remixed Festival was, for me, an experience like no other. It was the first time I was in spaces with large numbers of people who were of mixed race. I truly felt at home with these people, and fully understood for the first time. We shared numerous stories, and I met incredibly thoughtful and talented people from around the word. One mixed-race woman with whom I bonded came from Tokyo to attend the event and screen her documentary about the Japanese war brides. Another beautiful mixed-race family brought their east coast-based parents to attend as an anniversary gift.

I met the owner of BiracialBoom.com, an organization devoted to raising happy and healthy biracial children; Glenn Robinson, the founder of MixedAmericanLife.us, which curates and shares photos, articles and videos on the topics of mixed culture, mixed heritage and mixed identity, whether mixed by proximity, relationships, or adoption; actor Taye Diggs, who authored the children's book "Mixed Me," in honor of his mixed-race son; Thomas Lopez, the president of Multiracial Americans of Southern California, which has served the mixed-race community with resources, networking, workshops and community action since 1986;

and many other talented mixed-race poets, actors, authors, comedians, therapists, and students.

There were workshops on "The Dynamics of Interracial Relationships," "Tips and Talk About 'Biracial' Hair," "Multiracial and Families of Transracial Adoption in Conversation," "Mixed Millennials: Changing What Mixed-Race Means," "Mixed and Queer," among others. There were so many compelling workshops and presentations that I was disappointed I could not attend them all.

There were several dialogue circles organized for festival participants to share their mixed experiences. Many responded with sentiments about feeling safe and in kinship with others for the first time. It was a protective bubble, free from the hurts and microaggressions we all faced in the real world.

So what is it like out there? I amassed so many stories from those like me who don't fit neatly into racial or ethnic categories. I am a fifty-two-year-old female attorney of Filipino descent who has repeatedly been mistaken as the nanny of my own child. I have also been mistaken for a waitress at a country club and a secretary while I was an attorney at a large Washington law firm. When I started dating my husband in the late 1980s, his white grandparents saw my photo and asked if I could speak English. My experiences compare, and sometimes pale in comparison to those of others in mixed families.

My husband is primarily of Danish ancestry, and our son inherited his coloring. So my son does not look like me. That seems to throw people off.

The author, her son and then-husband

When I used to walk in our homogeneous Chevy Chase, Maryland, neighborhood, friendly nannies on the street asked me which household employs me. I did not take umbrage at their errors. However, at my son's Gymboree exercise class, the instructor asked me in front of the class if I had ever had a birthing experience. As my blue-eyed, fair-skinned son played on my lap and the rest of the Caucasian mothers looked on, I had to contain my annoyance as I responded that he was, in fact, my own son. I should not have to face such ignorance from a professional child educator at a class I was paying to attend.

When my children and I accompanied our next-door neighbor and her two blonde children to a local dentist to give my three-year-old a glimpse of what such a visit might be like, the dentist assumed that I was the nanny helping my neighbor out on this little excursion. As in the Gymboree class experience, I felt frustrated and demeaned.

At the time, I felt embarrassed and alone. There were not how-to books for parents of biracial children as there are today.[4]

I certainly am not alone. A sampling of the stories I heard:

—Phoebe Barnard's son resembles her Japanese-American husband. Barnard reports that people excitedly approach her with "Which country did you adopt him from?" "It's almost as if he's a hot commodity," says Barnard wryly.

---

4   See, e.g., Sharon Chang, *Raising Mixed Race: Multiracial Asian Children in a Post-Racial World* (Routledge, 2015); Marguerite Wright, *I'm Chocolate, You're Vanilla: Raising Healthy Black and Biracial Children in a Race-Conscious World* (Jossey-Bass, 2000); Donna Jackson-Nakazawa, *Does Anybody Else Look Like Me?: A Parent's Guide to Raising Multiracial Children* (Da Capo Press, 2004)

—Washington, D.C., mom Carol Bieberbach gets the adoption question about twice a month. Her husband hails from Haiti, and her children favor his side over her blonde, fair-skinned side of the family. When her husband came to their daughter's last dance class, another mother commented, "Oh, now it makes sense." Another woman in the local grocery store recently approached her with "Where did you get those children? I want to adopt a mixed-race child." Bieberbach usually replies that the children are "hers," but she seeks a better answer in deference to adopted children. She's come close to responding with the statement that her children were a "uterine experience."

—Nilmini Rubin's children have much lighter skin color than her. She was at the local park with her husband and their three children when a woman asked her how long she had been with the family. Rubin decided to answer, "Since the beginning." At the neighborhood swim club, "the woman behind the counter demanded that I show my nanny pass when I arrived with my kids. Having been members of the club for five years, this annoyed me, and I told her that 'I am not the nanny, I am the mom.' She approached me later that day to apologize, but somehow, this interaction stung."

—Barbara Tamialis, program director for All Saints All Day Preschool in Chevy Chase, Maryland, is a white woman with three adopted black children. Tamialis also has a white son. When with her black children, she finds that she receives extra scrutiny and even additional requests for identification when writing checks. People also frequently assume her small black son is lost when they walk next to each other at a mall. "What bothers me the most," Tamialis notes, however, "is the assumption that because my children are African-American, they are underprivileged and I am the benevolent white woman," something she witnesses at least annually during their fall school clothes shopping.

—Rocio Duty, an economist of Peruvian and Chinese descent, often hears "Is this your baby?" or "Are you the nanny?" when she is with her children, who resemble their Germanic father. Thus far, she is able to laugh off the comments or ignore them, chalking them up to ignorance on the part of the speakers.

—Helen, a white single parent from San Diego, was raised in South Dakota. Her family was uncomfortable with her decision to have children with a black man. Her sons, however, are relatively color-blind. "Race doesn't really seem to be an issue in Southern California, where we grew up. Our schools were very diverse."

—Kim Picca, a white woman who lives in Frederick, Maryland, adopted two boys from Ethiopia. Once, when one of her sons was lost, he described his mom as "the skinny pale one." Strangers laughed when they finally understood what he meant.

—Alison Bowman of Washington, D.C., affectionately calls her mixed-race daughter "swirly girl"; the Inadomi/Glaser children don't think about color or appearing different in Las Vegas, Nevada. They may look Asian, but they are as apple-pie-eating and baseball-playing as any of their peers. It has never come up in conversation. But Beverly Wong, a blonde Midwesterner, was frequently mistaken as the babysitter of her own Asian-looking children in Chevy Chase, Maryland.

From my numerous interviews with people of color, these experiences are not at all unusual. Unlike when I was feeling alone in my mixed-race experience, now there are Web sites where multiracial people gather online to connect and share resources.[5]

Of course, perhaps less spoken about are those who suffered much worse indignities. We hear about how black and part-black men live in fear, constantly keeping their guard up. Some I know have been "frisked for being black."[6]

One of my law school classmates was mistaken as a criminal trying to steal two white girls—his daughters—

5   See, for example, http://www.imnotthenanny.com and BiracialBoom.com

6   See, for example, winner of the 2015 National Book Award, *Between the World and Me* by Ta-Nehisi Coates (Spiegel & Grau, 2015)

from a Montgomery County, Maryland, park. Ironically, he was a prosecutor at the time who could have been called upon to prosecute such a crime.

Another girlfriend of color spoke of comments people made when she nursed her own white-looking baby. "That's disgusting," a white passerby once remarked.

A male friend who is black shared that his white wife's father from Richmond, Virginia, refused to attend the couple's wedding. Twenty years later, they are now civil to one another but not close.

Ninah Divine of Lake Geneva, Wisconsin, is the daughter of an African-American father and white mother of German, Norwegian, and Polish descent. Divine believes that "people are obsessed with race here. As an ethnically ambiguous person, they want me to have a narrative. I feel sexualized as the 'exotic other.'" Though her family doesn't discuss their multiracial identities much and raised her and her sister in diverse, liberal schools, she was told that when her mother announced to her family that she was dating her black father, her mother's father went into the bathroom and vomited.

Karen Smith of Richmond, Virginia, married a black man at a beautiful ceremony that her father refused to attend. She and her husband purposefully chose to send their children to diverse schools to avoid certain challenges.

Occasionally, she has faced questions from children asking why her skin color differs from that of her children. And once, someone asked Karen if her daughter were adopted. Her husband, DeMaurice, adds that "the toughest challenge is raising our kids with the hope of a color-blind world, while preparing them for one that is most certainly not. It is a strange duality, but one which I can only hope they understand one day. But my guess is they will only really appreciate it when it is their turn to raise their children."

Yahoo Parenting has many online stories from mixed race families:

> When Parks and Recreation star Rashida Jones corrected a reporter on the red carpet who complimented her "tan" by responding, "You know, I'm ethnic," I let out a knowing laugh. Ever since my half-Jewish (me), half-Puerto Rican (my husband) daughter was born, I've experienced many of those awkward exchanges with strangers. "Her skin is so dark! Were you just on vacation?" "She's so interesting… is she yours?" and the ever-popular "What is she?" I realize these inquiries ostensibly come from a place of innocent curiosity. After all, my child, especially as a baby, looked nothing like me, the pasty Goth chick with straight hair, yet was the spitting image of my swarthier, curly-headed husband. However, these questions reveal unpleasant societal assumptions

about what families are "supposed" to look like, and which kids and parents go together.

When you're just walking down the street and someone asks a question along those lines, it's jarring," Naomi Raquel Enright, a diversity associate at Horace Mann School in New York City tells Yahoo Parenting. Enright also deals with similar queries about her own mixed-heritage child. "My mother is from Ecuador and my dad was Jewish, and my husband is Irish and German," she says. "Our son has blond hair, blue eyes and light skin. He actually looks a lot like me if you get past his coloring, but many people don't see the resemblance. They think I'm the nanny. Once when someone asked, 'How long have you looked after him?' I said, 'Since he was in utero.'

I've heard similar stories from other friends with "ethnically ambiguous" children. When the white parent was with the child, the questions were of the "What is he?" variety. But when the parent of color was with the kid, the classist and racist conclusions were staggering. "When my sons were about one and two, I was pushing the double stroller out the front door of my building when a woman walked up to me and asked how much I charged to take care of the kids," Carol Cain, CEO of the blog Gone Girl Travel, and who is of Dominican-Puerto Rican heritage, tells Yahoo Parenting. "I looked at her confused, thinking that maybe I misheard her. It was the first time anyone had ever vocalized the perception that others might have about my biracial children not being mine because they were lighter-skinned and had green eyes."

With interracial marriages on the rise, the United States is more multicultural than ever, so I understand the curiosity—I often find myself wondering about people's ethnic backgrounds. But it's hard not to be defensive when asked if your child is, in fact, yours, especially when there are so few positive representations of interracial families in the media. And even when you find one—like in those wonderful Cheerios ads a few years back—there's backlash and controversy along with the support.

Yet I also believe that a question like "What is she?" can spark important conversations, which may lead to a deeper appreciation of our melting-pot culture. The trick is *how* the queries are asked and, perhaps more importantly, answered.

'It's all about approach and context,' says Enright. 'I'm much calmer now about those questions than when my son was a baby. Instead of feeling angry or upset, I just state the facts about who he is. I take it as a moment of illumination, how varied our histories are and how assumptions can be damaging. These may seem like harmless questions, but they're highlighting a whole other host of issues. It's important to prepare my son for these queries, that he has the tools to respond constructively and not feel bad about himself. My child is looking at me and how I answer. It's a teachable moment for him.'

Dr. Mariana Souto-Manning, professor of early childhood education at Columbia University and author of *Multicultural Teaching in the Early Childhood Classroom*, believes the key to demystifying interracial families is to discuss and celebrate differences from a young age. "A lot of early childhood teachers don't talk about race and identity because they think kids aren't ready, but children are already dealing with these micro-racial interactions every day," she tells Yahoo Parenting. "If we see every single one of us as a cultural being, we stop having this museum-walk perspective. It's important to start early or we're going to raise another generation of adults that have problematic ideas about race."

A mother of two herself, Souto-Manning answers bluntly when strangers inquire about her interracial children. "When somebody asks, 'Is he your child?' I say, 'You mean he doesn't look like me because he doesn't have brown skin?' I talk about it openly instead of being ashamed. Interracial marriage has only been [legal throughout the United States] since the late 1960s but attitudes didn't necessarily change right away. It wasn't until the '90s that the majority of people in the US thought interracial marriage was okay but there's not enough education about it."

Souto-Manning adds, "It's problematic because it shouldn't be up to us to educate the world. But entering conversations is a much more productive way to move ahead to dispel stereotypes so people can understand the beauty and diversity of our family."[7]

W. Ralph Eubanks, author of *The House at the End of the Road: The Story of Three Generations of an Interracial Family in the American South*,[8] writes eloquently about racial identity in his family. His mother had a white father and a black mother. She could "pass" for white, a notion that has "faded from American consciousness with the emergence of racial and multiracial pride." When she married a black man, she had to have her race as a white woman on her birth certificate changed to get a legal marriage certificate.

The Eubanks family of Washington, D.C.

---

7   https://www.yahoo.com/parenting/yes-shes-mine-and-no-shes-not-tan-shes-ethnic-110010433492.html

8   Smithsonian 2009

Eubanks describes a deep generational gulf between how he and his son considered racial identity, given the varying climate in which each grew up. Eubanks grew up "in a world of racial boundaries"; his son "grew up free of a repressive racial calculus." For his son, the traditional concept of race had been deconstructed. When his son was very young, Eubanks and his wife often fielded "what is he" questions and saw that many people assumed the son was adopted.

Eubanks and others note that our cultural mindset, tainted by the racial caste system of our past, is changing, albeit more slowly in certain parts of our country. Our binary system is becoming more fluid, largely by necessity, as our population becomes increasingly multicultural. Eubanks and others are educating people to a new way of thinking about race and identity. As these stories illustrate, change comes slowly as our assumptions become debunked.

Still, most of us assume in reading something, for instance, that the writer is talking about white people if there is no mention of race. I admit to that assumption, even though I am biracial, because I had become accustomed to race other than caucasian being noted in popular press.

The browning of America is very real and unrelenting. Our task is to find a way to move into this new "Ecru Era" with as much ease and grace as we can muster. There are no more completely white neighborhoods in America. An

April 2011 report from the Metropolitan Policy Program (MPP) at the Brookings Institution found that all but two of the ten largest metro areas in the country have child populations in which white children are a minority. (Boston and Philadelphia were the exceptions.) Of the remaining eight metro areas, Hispanic children are the largest demographic in six, and blacks are the largest in the other two. Brookings Institution demographer, William Frey, reported that in 1960, multiracial marriages constituted only 0.4 percent of all US marriages. That figure increased to 8.4 percent for recent newlyweds.[9]

The history of racism in our country has always seemed harsher towards black people. My own Asian mother expressed disdain for my dating African-American men, an attitude I find abhorrent, especially from a woman who came to this country for her postgraduate education and encountered rampant racism upon arrival. "Colorism,"[10] or people of color regarding lighter skin shade as preferable or somehow indicative of higher class, persists in many circles.

---

9   William H. Frey, "Multiracial Marriage on the Rise," December 18, 2014, Brookings.edu.

10 Colorism, or the dependence of social status based on skin color gradations alone, is a term originally attributed to author Alice Walker. "If the Present Looks Like the Past, What Does the Future Look Like?" from *In Search of Our Mothers' Gardens* (Harvest/Hbj. 1982), pages 290-91.

When I tan in the summer, my mother frequently berated me, remarking, "You look like a field-hand!"

Anastasia Bagliore, an African-American woman living in Potomac, Maryland, was raised in a wealthy Los Angeles neighborhood and married a white man, Alan, from Brooklyn. There was strong push back from her husband's father. "He was seventy-five at the time, old-world Italian, a retired construction brick layer, and not educated. His views were completely blue-collar American and also that of New York-Brooklyn-Queens. It was my first introduction to that type of person from those areas and totally in line with the social commentary movies I had seen by producers Spike Lee and Martin Scorsese. He said he couldn't accept it. Only when Alan told him that they no longer had anything to discuss—ever—and reminded him of his marriage to his mother who is Jewish—an interreligious marriage was much more controversial back in the 30s—did he begin to soften. Alan's father had forgotten how his in-laws did not acknowledge him and they crossed the street when they saw him in the neighborhood. Waterworks began, and he immediately apologized to me for three hours on the phone. When I gave birth to our son, he was his favorite grandchild, and I had a wonderful loving relationship with him after that. He also told Alan many years later that I was the best decision he ever made. I find that the more worldly, wealthy, educated, and sophisticated people don't blink an eye. Their world is global. I will also say that stereotypes exist because they are true! I had to remind the Brooklyn group that I grew up in far more superior circumstances, with more travel, better education, and more opportunities than they could imagine. That was, and still is, a bitter pill to swallow."

Certainly, our country's attitudes are evolving. The same-sex right to marry fight parallels that of mixed-race marriage. When I told my children about the fact that it was illegal for my parents to marry in 1961 in Maryland, they were incredulous. When they tell their children some day that their dads couldn't marry in Maryland in 2014, their children will also find that hard to believe.

In 1970s suburban Maryland, I was the only mixed-race person I knew. My grade school was a sea of white. A neighborhood boy repeatedly taunted me with remarks about rice paddies. People kept asking me if my parents had met during the war. I can still conjure up the sting of being excluded from the "freckle club" of my third grade. Like so many other children, I just wanted to be like everyone else. I was a "closeted Asian."[11] It wasn't until I was in my twenties that I reveled in my uniqueness.

Flash forward four decades. Mixed race couples are de rigueur. The year 2014 marks the fiftieth anniversary

---

11 http://www.swirlinc.org/, August 20, 2012, "Dinner With Choi"

of *McLaughlin v. Florida*, the Supreme Court decision that overturned a Florida law prohibiting interracial cohabitation (this was three years before *Loving v. Virginia*, in which the court overturned state laws prohibiting interracial marriage).[12] That case was triggered when Dora Goodnick, the landlady of a white woman named Connie Hoffman, called the police to report that a black fellow was spending a lot of time in her tenant's apartment. Hoffman and her Honduran-born boyfriend, Dewey McLaughlin, were tried for violating Florida law and sentenced to thirty days of hard labor. With the help of the NAACP Legal Defense Fund, they fought the conviction.

A lot has changed in fifty years. According to the *Los Angeles Times*, 9 percent of unmarried couples living together in 2012 came from different races. And the number of married and unmarried interracial couples has more than doubled since 2000, the *Times* reports.[13] Witness the increasingly common commercials, Blue Cross Blue Shield, and Verizon Web site home pages, and two-

---

12   In honor of the anniversary, National Public Radio conducted a month of exploring interracial and cross-cultural romance in a show called *Code Switch*. See http://www.npr.org/sections/codeswitch/2014/01/15/262731129/in-search-of-great-questions-about-cross-cultural-romance

13   Emily Alpert, "Interracial Couples Increasingly Common, Though Many Aren't Marrying," *Los Angeles Times*, August 31, 2013.

story high fashion billboards peppered around New York City featuring now somewhat typical mixed-race couples and families.

As Eubanks points out, "Race continues to divide American culture, even as we have come to accept a more fluid concept of race and ethnicity. We agree that what divides groups are the assumptions each makes about the other's experiences, assumptions that are ingrained from childhood, depending on what our families teach us, by word or example. But we are optimistic that at some point in the future, Americans could move toward a concept of race and ethnicity with more bridges than boundaries." We can hope.

Families Led
by Same-Sex Couples

You're so lucky to have two mommies!

—First grader to his classmate,
Silver Spring, Maryland

American attitudes toward same-sex marriage have changed at lightening speed. Just a decade ago, more than six in ten Americans opposed the right of same-sex couples to marry. Those numbers have now flipped. In 2015, ABC News/*The Washington Post* released their latest poll, showing that 61 percent of Americans support same-sex marriage and 35 percent do not.[1] The pollsters called it "a dramatic, decade-long evolution in public attitudes on gay marriage—one of the most remarkable re-evaluations of views on a basic social issue in more than 30 years of ABC/Post polling."

---

1   http://www.langerresearch.com/wp-content/uploads/
    1144a49GayMarriage.pdf

Appendix Table 3. Interracial/Interethnic
Same-Sex Couple Households: 2010

Type of Couple	Number	Percent
TOTAL same-sex couple households 2010	646,464	
Total same race or same Hispanic origin couples	512,987	
Total interracial/interethnic couples	133,477	100.0
White non-Hispanic/Hispanic (any race)	56,632	42.4
White non-Hispanic/Black non-Hispanic	17,475	13.1
White non-Hispanic/AIAN non-Hispanic	5,087	3.8
White non-Hispanic/Asian non-Hispanic	15,110	11.3
White non-Hispanic/NHPI non-Hispanic	997	0.7
White non-Hispanic/SOR non-Hispanic	919	0.7
Both are multiracial, (both Hispanic or neither Hispanic)	4,001	3.0
Hispanic/non-Hispanic (excluding White non-Hispanic)	10,549	7.9
Other-both Hispanic (partners different single race, neither White)	501	0.4
Other-neither Hispanic (partners different single race, neither White)	1,447	1.1

Appendix Table 3. Interracial/Interethnic
Same-Sex Couple Households: 2000

Type of Couple	Number	Percent
TOTAL same-sex couple households 2000	594,391	
Total same race or same Hispanic origin couples	511,200	
Total interracial/interethnic couples	83,191	100.0
White non-Hispanic/Hispanic (any race)	30,872	37.1
White non-Hispanic/Black non-Hispanic	10,234	12.3
White non-Hispanic/AIAN non-Hispanic	4,220	5.1
White non-Hispanic/Asian non-Hispanic	7,780	9.4
White non-Hispanic/NHPI non-Hispanic	702	0.8
White non-Hispanic/SOR non-Hispanic	585	0.7
Both are multiracial, (both Hispanic or neither Hispanic)	6,690	8.0
Hispanic/non-Hispanic (excluding White non-Hispanic)	5,679	6.8
Other-both Hispanic (partners different single race, neither White)	363	0.4
Other-neither Hispanic (partners different single race, neither White)	1,054	1.3

Interracial and Interethnic Coupled Households Appendix
Tables Households and Families: 2010 Census Brief
http://www.census.gov/population/www/
cen2010/briefs/tables/appendix.pdf

Germantown, Maryland, family, Michael
and Khang Sharp and their son

In 1961, being gay was officially classified as a mental disorder.[2] From 2000 to 2010, however, the number of same-sex unmarried partner households almost doubled, according to the US Census figures.[3] Undoubtedly aware of the trend, the iconic Campbell's Soup Company in October 2015 released a television commercial nationwide featuring two gay fathers. While there was some backlash from

---

2   National Public Radio, July 1, 2015, show on the film, *The Rejected*.

3   There were 358,000 same-sex unmarried partner households in 2000, increasing to 646,000 in the 2010 census. In 2000, same-sex unmarried partner households accounted for 0.3 percent of all households, doubling in proportion to 0.6 percent of all households in 2010. http://www.census.gov/prod/cen2010/briefs/c2010br-14.pdf, page 15.

people who implored Campbell's to "stay out of the cultural wars," cultural norms—and numbers—are changing.

Perhaps that is why Hillary Clinton's 2015 campaign launch video includes a same-sex couple discussing their wedding plans and hope for the Supreme Court ruling to end discriminatory laws prohibiting same-sex marriage. Gay people have political, economic, and social influence today. The stigma is quickly eroding.

Perhaps Hillary is braver than I. When my parents got married in 1961, interracial marriages were illegal in sixteen states. They lived in Maryland, but they had to go to the District of Columbia to get married. My children are incredulous when I tell them this. I believe their children will be surprised when we tell them that same-sex marriage was illegal in many states in 2014. While the tide is turning, the "mama bear" in me doesn't want my gay son to spend time in the south—at least not in rural areas. I still am haunted by the notorious Matthew Shepard murder in 1998 while he was a college student in Wyoming. I know anti-gay hate crimes can occur anywhere, but my experience of racism in the south has made me more wary of it.

The critically acclaimed NBC television show *Will and Grace* broke cultural ground in 1998 by featuring an openly gay male character on prime time television. It was credited with helping and improving public opinion of the LGBT community, with US Vice President Joe Biden commenting that the show "probably did more to educate the American public" on LGBT issues "than almost anything anybody has ever done so far."[4]

Twenty-five years ago, a children's picture book *Heather Has Two Mommies*,[5] caused a huge splash. After fifty publishers turned it down, its publishing became a cultural and legal flashpoint, angering conservatives over the morality of same-sex parenting and landing libraries at the center of community battles. Now, the publishing landscape has been transformed. Author Leslea Newman recently updated the book with an important but subtle change—the two mommies are wearing wedding bands.

During the writing of this book, the United States Supreme Court overturned the Defense of Marriage Act in a landmark ruling, enabling gay couples throughout our country to marry legally. Starbucks was one of the more than three hundred US corporations that signed the Supreme Court brief against the Defense of Marriage Act. The right to marry for gay couples is the law of the land.

Most of us know gay couples either in our families or among our friends and work colleagues. Famous gay people

---

4   http://www.washingtontimes.com/news/2012/may/6/biden-will-grace-educated-public-about-gays/

5   (Alyson Books, 1989); (Candlewick, 2015)

have been around for ages—Alvin Ailey, Joan Baez, James Beard, Leonard Bernstein, Truman Capote, Anderson Cooper, Jodie Foster, Barney Frank, Neil Patrick Harris, Jasper Johns, Annie Leibovitz, Greg Louganis, Rosie O'Donnell, Herb Ritts, David Sedaris, Maurice Sendack, Alice Walker, and Walt Whitman, to name a few. Elton John and Liberace were out before it was widely accepted, and their careers didn't suffer for it. Leading man Rock Hudson was not permitted to be out when he was in his prime acting days. But today, leading comedian and gay rights advocate Ellen DeGeneres is outrageously popular.

Gay families are going mainstream. In 2004, *The Washington Post* featured a story on its Kidspost page about a ten-year-old boy with two moms. In the story, the child, Justin, says it doesn't feel like a big deal being in this kind of household. Their daily routine is much like any family's. The *Post* reported in this article that "families like Justin's are not unique…Still, a majority of Americans remain uncomfortable with the idea of same-sex marriage."[6]

Betsy Keteltas of Tavernier, Florida, feared that her Massachusetts-based parents would not approve of her marriage to another woman. "It took me many, many years to realize that the most important ingredient in my family was the love they had for each one of us. This may have

---

6   Fern Shen, "Defining Marriage," *The Washington Post*, March 17, 2004.

been a bit gray during the years I was coming out, the years where they were adjusting. Geography—distance—helped quite a bit. It gave all of us the space to figure things out. We all made excuses for each other when we behaved poorly. 'Mom and Dad were born in a different generation, so don't expect them to change their thoughts. It will take years.' This seemed like the most common comment among families with older parents. These days, that's ancient history. A week before I got married, I broke the news to my parents. We hadn't invited them to the wedding because we made the assumption they did not want to attend. What resulted was the most healing moment. Both my mom and my dad shared with me that they were sorry for how they had treated me over the years, that they love me, that they loved my wife, and that they were happy for me."

© Scott Griessel

Memphis residents Lindsey and Micaela Watts had the immediate support of their family but have "been met with some blatant stares of disgust before. We spend a lot of our time in the more progressive part of Memphis, the blue epicenter if you will, so we haven't experienced much prejudice. What is more likely to happen, and has happened many times, is to be met with inappropriate cheering and/or verbal encouragement from heterosexual males when showing public affection. To me, that is just as inexcusable, as though we exist and love one another just for the voyeuristic kicks some dude is getting out of it." The couple would like to have children together, but Micaela worries greatly that the cost will be prohibitive. "You have to really, really want and carefully plan to have children if you are a same-sex couple," Watts maintains. "Without a doubt, the most angering and frustrating thing about being gay in this country is that there is still an amazingly large percentage of the population that thinks that this is a lifestyle choice. And that brilliant logic always comes from a self-professed straight person. It blows my damn mind how people—and politicians especially—feel so confident in speaking for someone else's experience. That is still the most dangerous lie out there. Something happens to you when a very honest and intimate part of your being is debated on a daily basis on countless platforms. When a citizen and/or a Supreme Court is given the right to vote on whether you are allowed to exist as you are, the way you were created, something very dark grows in your psyche, and overpowering this anger, for me, is a daily struggle."

Karen Ahlers of Ashland, Massachusetts, had children many years apart and had very differing experiences raising them as our cultural climate changed. "My experiences raising Kyle twenty years ago were very different than my more recent experiences raising Tucker. Gay rights have evolved dramatically in the last ten years. When Kyle began nursery school at age four, one of the parents complained to the school director that gay families should not be permitted in the school. The director told her she was narrow-minded. Several years later, the director told us that the parent reported having spoken to other parents, who all said we were 'very nice people' and that the woman was now embarrassed about her comments of a few years before."

"When Kyle was ten, the antigay marriage groups were collecting signatures to try to ban gay marriage in Massachusetts. When we noticed a man collecting signatures at our local supermarket, Kyle, her best friend Michaela, and I told people that we lived in the town and asked people to consider not signing his petition. When people stopped signing his petition, he became enraged at us and told Kyle and Michaela that I was a child abuser. When we didn't leave, he told us that he was going to follow us home. Then he told us he was going to 'call the police on us,' which he did. Once the police realized what was happening, they escorted him from the parking lot. It was scary."

"We didn't have any similar experiences with Tucker. The outright hostility toward gays has dissipated in the last few years. But the antigay slurs continue. 'That's so gay' and 'you're such a fag' are widely used in high schools, including in Tucker's school. These terms are usually not meant to hurt gay people, but they do, of course. The harm is insidious and subtle, but each time a gay person hears it, the message is clear. There is something wrong with them. And it's not just gay people that are harmed by these innocuous slurs. It's people who aren't sure if they are gay, or friends of gay people. It's family members of gay people. It's straights who have physical attributes generally associated with gay people. It's straights who might want to participate in an activity generally thought of as natural for the other sex, like boys who like to cook, sing, or dance, or girls who want to box or wrestle. Really, the list of who is harmed by these slurs is endless, but our teens use them daily. They have terrible vocabularies, for one thing. There are usually ten more descriptive adjectives or adverbs which could be used in place of gay. And kids don't realize how many people around them are negatively affected by gay slurs. Parents really aren't doing their jobs. They fail to have conversations with their children, and allow them to use these slurs. If they heard their children call someone a nigger, they would have a conversation with the child and make sure they understand why this term is unacceptable. But they don't do this when they hear their children say 'That's so gay.'

"So I guess I would say that harm to gay people isn't as obvious as it was a decade ago. It is more subtle. But it exists. It hurts just as much as some of the more shocking incidents. But hearing gay used as a negative description for one's entire life has consequences."

The Ahlers/Olsen family of Ashland, Massachusetts

Kate Olsen, Karen's wife, who has two younger sons from a prior marriage, has no negative stories to share about her parenting experiences. She cites her progressive state of Massachusetts and involvement in the Unitarian Universalist Church as two reasons for this.

"My kids have never been the only kids of gay parents in any of their classes at school. No one has batted an eye, even with the new family constellation which now includes a stepmother, stepsiblings, and all of the extended family members that are involved in our lives. My kids have been very blessed to have so many adults in their lives who love them and offer endless support. They have not experienced anything that would make them think their family is any different than anyone else's. They know plenty of kids whose parents are divorced. Their friends are aware that they go back and forth between my house and their other mother's house and simply ask matter-of-factly where they are going to be that weekend in case they want to get together."

Marie, who grew up in Florida but now lives in Boston, was disowned by her parents when she came out at age sixteen. Her parents sent her to "conversion therapy." Now, she has been married to a woman for four years, and they have three children. There was no pushback from either of their extended families, but they were very interested in the particulars of how they got pregnant (something they decided to keep between themselves). However, she chooses to live in the northeast because of southern conservatism she witnessed. "We wanted to ensure that [our children] would have the easiest upbringing possible. Our children didn't choose to have two moms.... We wanted to make sure we lived in an area that is open and accepting of our family as well as having a strong community of LGBT families. People's mindsets have shifted greatly from a generation ago, but not enough where I would raise a child with gay parents in Florida.

"At the hospital, when my wife was giving birth to our daughter, we were treated like any other couple having their first child. The nurses and midwives laughed and cried with us, and supported us as a couple and as new parents," Marie says. "They told us stories of other first time parents that have come through the hospital, in effect normalizing our family, because that's what we are—normal. My wife and I love each other and we love the children that we made together. Love is what makes a family and we've got lots of it. In that sense, we are no different than any other family. I know that we will eventually face some type of pushback or prejudice because I don't think our society has progressed that far. But we are just like any other couple figuring out this great thing called motherhood."

Michael and Khang of Germantown, Maryland, recently adopted a baby boy. They knew having a child would change their lives, but they never expected the extent of the change. "We have been together for twelve years and married for ten years. Growing our family through adoption has changed our relationship in incredible ways that we never expected. It has changed our relationship with our extended family and close friends and brought other friends into our lives that we would never have met before. Also, we knew that whatever child we ended up with we would love with all of our hearts; we just didn't realize how strong that love would be." They have many friends with children and so far have not experienced criticism or ostracism as gay parents. Only love.

Assumptions change as differences become more common, "normalized," in our collective experience. A generation ago, many gay people would remain closeted their entire lives. Jim of Mendham, New Jersey, was married to a beautiful woman for twenty-one years with whom he had three children before the weight of his secret became too heavy for him to bear. "While we all still struggle with things, we have forged a new normal, and I dare say that everyone is thriving!"

Gay families are all over the Internet. The LGBT wedding and LGBT-friendly vacation industries are big business.[7] For example, a northern California family headed by two gay men have started making YouTube videos to show that gay families are no different than straight families in valuing marriage and family. "We hope these images of happy LGBT families from all around the world will destroy some of the negative stereotypes about gay families."[8]

---

7   See, e.g., equallywed.com, thelgbtexpo.com, deltavacations. com/info/lgbt-vacations, and iglta.org

8   See Gay Family Values https://www.youtube.com/user/depfox. See also http://www.huffingtonpost.com/gay-voices, and http://www.lgbtqnation.com.

A *New York Times* article on work-life balance quotes Randy Florke, founder of Rural Connection, an interior design and construction firm in New York describing delegation of duties with his husband, Sean Patrick Maloney, a US congressman.[9] Together, they have three children, ages twelve, fourteen, and twenty-five, living at home. While I did a mental double take on the article's pronouns—rereading the words "his husband," as a reference to an elected official, it is not likely that my children would stumble reading that. In fact, my daughter is in a college class where pronouns are avoided. Both my high-school-aged son and college-aged daughter have friends and acquaintances who prefer no gender pronouns to be used when referring to them. My son's boarding school has a dedicated dorm for transgender individuals and others who wish to live in a gender-neutral dorm. Unlike my children, I must work on my biases and be mindful of assumptions I have made in the past because of the society and time in which I grew up. At some point in our children's lifetimes, for example, media may not commonly refer to those who are non-white or non-heterosexual with racial or sexual orientation qualifiers.

Despite increasing acceptance of gay people by our society at large, I worry as the parent of a gay son. Upon

---

9   Paul Sullivan, "Work-Life Balance Poses Challenges Regardless of Wealth" *New York Times*, October 9, 2015.

learning that my son was gay, a woman at my Washington, D.C., Catholic church, with whom I had been in a prayer group years ago, remarked to me, "What a cross you and your son bear. Same-sex unions are anathema to God. I urge you to look for a good priest to help you and your family. I'll be keeping you in my prayers." And I pray for her. I pray that such misguided narrow-mindedness is eradicated quickly from our society, and that acceptance of all continues to grow.

Single Parents— Those Who Choose to Go It Alone

While skimming through my Facebook newsfeed one morning in April 2015, a site called "Single Mothers by Choice" came across the screen. I knew several professional women who became mothers via sperm donors, but it seemed relatively rare.

This decade, however, has witnessed a steep rise in women choosing single motherhood. Many of the women I interviewed focused on their careers during their prime childbearing years and came to parenting relatively late in life. Medical advances have enabled women of this generation to become pregnant via sperm donors. And the choice has gained popularity in our culture.

A recent documentary, "Chill: A Modern-Day Journey to Motherhood," chronicles a single woman's fight during her mid-30s to preserve her fertility and dreams of motherhood via egg freezing, with or without a partner. The director, actress Jennifer Frappier, won sponsorship of the project by the New York Foundation for the Arts and debuted the film at the Mixed Remixed Festival in Los Angeles in June of 2016.

The documentary is honest, raw and brave. As Frappier notes, "Egg freezing is a proactive choice. It doesn't mean you've failed....Women need to be educated on their fertility while they have time to preserve it. If we can adjust from teaching young women pregnancy prevention and educate them about their fertility as a whole, the ticking clock will become less of an issue."[1]

In 1994, when Tamar Abrams, a single mother in North Arlington, Virginia, penned an article on her becoming a single mother "by choice," she received hate mail and furious telephone calls.[2] She had learned about sperm banks and was refused service by one because she was single. Twenty years later, she marvels that her sperm bank supplier has "donor-matching consultants" who will compare potential donors' photos to pictures of your relatives. And another in the Washington area has "FaceMatch" technology whereby patrons can match characteristics electronically of photos to potential donors.

Perhaps the decade's steep rise in women who choose single motherhood has to do with media portrayals. Perhaps it has to do with female empowerment. Hollywood stars Sandra Bullock and Cameron Diaz are doing it. Halle Berry does it.

---

1   www.chillthedocumentary.com

2   "Just the Two of Us," *Washingtonian* magazine, August 2013.

Perhaps *Murphy Brown* started the trend years ago. Or at least brought it to the forefront of our nation's psyche. *Murphy Brown*, the titular character of which was played onscreen by Candice Bergen, was a popular show in the '80s and '90s. Brown was funny and confident and embodied the type of woman which many of us aspired to be.

Then–Vice President Quayle used Murphy Brown's decision to be a single mom as a campaign platform. "Vice President Quayle dared to argue last week in a San Francisco speech that the Los Angeles riots were caused in part by a 'poverty of values' that included the acceptance of unwed motherhood, as celebrated in popular culture by the CBS comedy series *Murphy Brown*," reported Isabel Sawhill of *The Washington Post*.

> On May 19, 1992, as the presidential campaign season was heating up, Vice President Dan Quayle delivered a family-values speech that came to define him nearly as much as his spelling talents. Speaking at the Commonwealth Club of California, he chided Murphy Brown—the fictional 40-something, divorced news anchor played by Candice Bergen on a CBS sitcom—for her decision to have a child outside of marriage.
>
> 'Bearing babies irresponsibly is simply wrong,' the vice president said. 'Failing to support children one has fathered is wrong. We must be unequivocal about this. It doesn't help matters when prime time

TV has Murphy Brown, a character who supposedly epitomizes today's intelligent, highly paid professional woman, mocking the importance of fathers by bearing a child alone and calling it just another lifestyle choice.'

Quayle's argument—that Brown was sending the wrong message, that single parenthood should not be encouraged—erupted into a major campaign controversy. And just a few weeks before the '92 vote, the show aired portions of his speech and had characters react to it.

'Perhaps it's time for the vice president to expand his definition and recognize that, whether by choice or circumstance, families come in all shapes and sizes,' Bergen's character said.

Her fictional colleague Frank, meanwhile, echoed some of the national reaction: 'It's Dan Quayle—forget about it!'

Twenty years later, Quayle's words seem less controversial than prophetic. The number of single parents in America has increased dramatically: the proportion of children born outside marriage has risen from roughly 30 percent in 1992 to 41 percent in 2009. For women under age 30, more than half of babies are born out of wedlock. A lifestyle once associated with poverty has become mainstream. The only group of parents for whom marriage continues to be the norm is the college-educated. Twenty years later, it turns out Dan Quayle was right about Murphy Brown and unmarried moms.[3]

Media portrayals make it look easy. It's not.

Sue, an accomplished Los Angeles attorney, decided to adopt a baby on her own. Though raised in a traditional east coast family, she was confident she could raise a child on her own and was sure she wanted a baby. She hadn't anticipated how difficult it would be.

"I had no time for myself," Sue said when asked of the biggest challenge of single parenting. "I'd come home from a demanding day at work, and my babysitter would hand me the baby."

Los Angeles family, Sue and her child

---

3   Isabel Sawhill, "20 Years Later, It Turns Out Dan Quayle Was Right About Murphy Brown and Unmarried Moms," *The Washington Post*, May 25, 2012.

Sue was frazzled for several years and finally left her high-powered entertainment industry job to become a full-time, at-home mom. Technology, at least for some types of jobs, allows parents the ability to do some work while being at home. Sue hopes that when she reenters the workforce, she will find a flexible company that will allow her to telecommute for part of her work.

Sue also laments not having someone to bounce ideas off of with regard to raising her child or someone with whom to share her child's precious moments. In addition, she finds that other local parents she knows prefer to socialize with other couples, not a single mom.

"My daughter is the only kid without a dad in our public school," Sue asserts.[4] She winces when she hears other children asking her daughter about her daddy.

But Sue and her daughter are very close, and they work together to make things work for them, which gets easier

---

4   Interestingly, in my daughter's Catholic, all-girls school in Bethesda, Maryland, there were two students in her small grade alone who were raised by single women with no father in the picture. No one knew who the girls' fathers were, and no one asked or regarded it as odd. Much has been written about absent fathers in underprivileged neighborhoods, of course. But raising a child alone by choice seems to becoming a more mainstream path today.

as her daughter ages. "It's just me and Katie against the world," Sue declares.

Another single mother, Michele Arington, a lawyer in Arlington, Virginia, didn't want to wait for the right person to come along to start a family. When she was ready to have a child, she was ready. "Now's the time," Arington said. At age thirty-seven, Arington gave birth to her daughter, and she never looked back.

Arington is matter-of-fact about the matter. She is unfazed by others' comments or questions and knows she has made a life that is right for her and for her daughter.

She admits that other children expressed curiosity when Arington's daughter was younger. "You don't have a daddy?" they'd ask. "But you have to have a daddy!" they'd insist. "No, you don't," her daughter would respond with an eye roll.

Lynn Buchanan, from Birmingham, Alabama, got pregnant and chose not to marry the father of her child. She moved close to her parents, who provided support as Lynn raised her daughter alone. Lynn recalls no insensitive comments or feeling isolated or different because of their small family unit. Lynn's daughter was a happy child and enjoys a very close relationship with her mother, perhaps even closer, as she grew up without siblings or a father in her day-to-day life.

The Facebook page of professional photographer, Marissa Rauch, of Washington, D.C., is peppered with joyful photos of her daughter and various milestones in their lives. It is apparent that Marissa and her daughter have abundant family and friends with which to celebrate.

Washington, D.C., family Marissa Rauch and her daughter

"I always wanted to be a mother and I promised myself at age 35 that I would not be 40 without a child," Rauch remembers. "I just knew I wanted to be a mom and did not want it to pass me by."

Rauch used Adoptions Together to adopt her baby from Russia, and at the time it took about ten months. "I was very lucky because it takes much much longer now. I only had to go to Russia one time. Now you cannot even adopt from Russia.

"I never thought we were different than other families. I have many friends and we are all just moms, whether we are married or not. We talk about our kids, have fun, etc. Choosing to be a single mom was not nearly as common as it is today. I did not know anyone else who chose to do it on their own at that time. So, I just hung around with my friends and all the families including mine would and still get together as families.

"It is hard to be the sole supporter of my family. I have to be really organized to balance my business, my daughter and our life. But I have amazing support—a wonderful family, especially my mother and my sister who are essential and totally involved in my life and my daughter's. I have incredible friends who add so much to our life in so many ways. We are extremely lucky to have so many supportive people in our lives.

"I always refer to myself as 'pre-Angelina.' because I adopted as a single person when it was pretty unusual. After Angelina Jolie adopted, it was in the news a lot more and much more common. It is so common today, not unusual at all. If you look at the stats and see how many households are run by single parents, it is astounding. It is more the norm these days."

Cheverly, Maryland resident Alison Alverado had her daughter Maya in 2007. There was no pushback from her extended family or friends. She finds she has a large community of support. Maya has known from early in her life that she has a donor as her biological father. In fact, she knows ten other children fathered by the same donor. When she was smaller, she wanted to make the donor Father's Day gifts. "I explained that he was a guy who donated the gift of life to her, but he was not her father," says Alverado. "She's had the opportunity to meet and visit with her biological half-siblings and they are very close when they are together and quite loving. She hasn't asked about the donor since she's met and spent time with her siblings." Alverado posits that, as time goes on, the definitions of family grow. "I think the Internet allows people to share a closeness that may not have been as noticeable in the past."

Clare Jacocks, a single mom in Kensington, Maryland, views her status as unremarkable. "My single parent status has just been my norm. I haven't made it complicated nor do I compare it to others or the world. If anyone ever had anything negative to say, I never heard it. Either it was behind my back or I just don't listen for it."

Jane of Buck's County, Pennsylvania, expressed a similar sentiment. "I just did what I had to do," she declares. The birth father was too unstable to parent, so Jane raised her son alone. The all-white community in which she lived presented some challenges for her and her biracial son, but they weathered the storm together. Her son now is a highly successful banker in New York City.

Many people parenting alone, of course, do not choose to have it that way. Marie, of Wilmington, Delaware, is from a large family and wanted her daughter to have siblings. A divorce ended that dream for her.

As her daughter heads off for college, Marie reflects:

> "I can't even believe I made it this far. It has been financially difficult to provide for her as I wanted to. I was one hundred percent committed to her, so I had very little social life. I just did what I had to do. I'm stubborn, an I-can-do-it-myself kind of person. It was just hard. I now mentor other women going through similar things.
>
> "Unlike when my parents divorced and I was bullied and not invited to various things because of it, my daughter has not suffered because of my divorce. It is all she knows, and she has friends whose parents divorced as well.
>
> "My own mother was not able to deal with the crisis in her life. I feel like I have done a good job with my daughter. While I am looking forward to having more time for me, I wouldn't change one second of the time I had with my daughter."

Women, of course, are not the only parents raising their children alone. Doug of Dayton, Ohio, did not want that for his daughter, but had little choice. Doug and the birth-mother met while seeking treatment for alcoholism and addiction, but his girlfriend could not stay sober, even after their baby was born.

It was not an easy road for this single father. "Chronic fatigue was my closest friend," Doug says. "I would have had seven children," but not with my daughter's birth-mother." Doug did not date for many years, because all of his focus was on his daughter, his job and his own sobriety. He found a job that allowed him to be home when school was out. His close female friends were very supportive and helpful. "I could never repay the debt I have to the women in the [Alcoholics Anonymous] program. A woman's love is softer and different. These women helped me learn the ropes of caring for a daughter."

"Out of my struggles, I help a lot of other men going through similar things," Doug notes. "I've had a chance to mentor a lot of men parenting alone. My daughter was a catalyst for my sobriety. This little girl saved my life."

Kevin, a Baltimore resident, raised his two sons alone. His former wife was a drug addict and incapable of caring for the boys. Kevin is a hands-on father, frequently showing up at the schools to help his sons and other fatherless boys. He became a surrogate father to many of the children in the neighborhood. While he, like other single parents, faced significant challenges, the payoff was worth it.

....

In 2011, Kate Bolick charted the sea change in our cultural attitudes toward marriage in her *Atlantic* cover story, "All the Single Ladies." Interweaving personal experience—she was thirty-nine and single at the time—with reporting, Bolick noted that we are marrying later or not at all, with many women exercising their ability to have children without partners or, again, not at all.[5] The piece generated a huge response.[6] But would it do so in 2016? Unlikely.

---

5   Kate Bolick, "All the Single Ladies" *The Atlantic*, November, 2011.

6   In Bolick's new book, *Spinster: Making a Life of One's Own*, she approaches single adulthood from a slightly different angle. The book is part memoir and describes her breaking away from a serious, cohabitating relationship in her late twenties, exploring her ambivalence about partnership, and wholly reconsidering her view of marriage. Along the way, she presents the stories of her five "awakeners," the historical single women who shaped her thinking. These were the essayist Maeve Brennan, the poet Edna St. Vincent Millay, the columnist Neith Boyce, the novelist Edith Wharton, and the writer and activist Charlotte Perkins Gilman. By considering these women's biographies and cultural contexts, Bolick began to better understand her own.

Parents of Singletons

"One is enough."

—John Decker,
Brooklyn, New York

When I was a child growing up in a predominantly Catholic neighborhood in suburban Washington, D.C., everyone I knew had siblings—lots of them. We felt sorry for "only" children we heard about or came across. Only children were often maligned as spoiled, maladjusted, or bossy. One generation later and my daughter's elementary school classes had numerous families in which there was only one child.

Perhaps our most famous contemporary American family with one child is the Clintons. Hillary Clinton was asked about it by the press—isn't having only one child unusual?[1] "But I just didn't have any more children," Clinton replied. "Not that I didn't *want* any more." Other famous solo children include Mahatma Gandhi, Indira Gandhi, Condoleezza Rice, Lauren Bacall, Betty White, Kareem

---

1   Rachel Combe, "At the Pinnacle of Hillary Clinton's Career," *Elle*, April 15, 2012.

Abdul-Jabbar, Robert De Niro, Samuel L. Jackson, Tommy Lee Jones, Al Pacino, Matthew Perry, Sammy Davis Jr., Daniel Radcliffe, Danielle Steele, Charlize Theron, and Rudy Giuliani.

"Only-child families are becoming the new traditional family, for a number of reasons," says social psychologist and author Susan Newman, PhD. Dr. Newman observes that many women are having children later in life and that more and more families are concerned about the cost of raising children.

With these demographic and economic trends and research that indicates only children aren't disadvantaged at all—and may have an edge in certain areas—it is not hard to understand why single-child families are growing at a faster rate than families with more than one child, Newman says.

Singleton children, in fact, often fare better than those with siblings. Although this phenomenon has long been observed, there was little conclusive data on why only children seem to possess such an advantage. A new study sheds some light on the issue, particularly demonstrating the higher academic success and educational aspirations for such individuals.[2]

2   Bu, F. (2014). "Sibling Configuration, Educational Aspiration and Attainment." Institute for Social and Economic Research,

Dr. Newman writes a column for *Psychology Today* on the world of singleton children.[3] She penned two books on the subject: *The Case for The Only Child*[4] and *Parenting an Only Child: The Joys and Challenges of Raising Your One and Only.*[5] Dr. Newman has studied families with solo children since the 1980s and writes about battling negative stereotypes, resisting pressure to have more children, and offers advice to families with "onlies." According to Newman:

> Those who study demographics agree that the one-child household is the fastest-growing family unit. It surprises many people to learn that one-child families outnumber families with two children and have for more than a decade. Fertility rates in many places are dropping rapidly, especially in the richest countries, where, to put it simply, any two people are not producing two more people. There are a number of explanations for this trend. People marry later, leaving them fewer childbearing years and a greater chance of facing infertility or secondary infertility;

2014-11. https://www.iser.essex.ac.uk/research/publications/working-papers/iser/2.

3   https://www.psychologytoday.com/blog/singletons

4   Susan Newman, PhD, *The Case for The Only Child* (HCI, 2011)

5   Susan Newman, PhD, *Parenting an Only Child: The Joys and Challenges of Raising Your One and Only* (Broadway Books, 2001)

more and more people opt to have and raise a child as single parents and one is realistically all they can handle; one out of almost every two marriages ends in divorce, often before a second child is considered or born, and predictions are that divorce rates will not change much in the foreseeable future.[6]

TIME magazine contributor Jeffrey Kluger agrees that only children have advantages over children with siblings. "Only children tend to wind up with a better vocabulary and a more sophisticated sense of humor, simply because they grow up in a house outnumbered by parents," he says.[7]

On the other hand, many only children I spoke with cited feelings of loneliness or that they were missing out on the sibling experience. Julie Chrisco Andrews of Washington, D.C., was an only child and birthed an only child. "One of the worst things about being an only child is that when my mother died, it all fell on my shoulders," Andrews says. "It has made me very sad that I have left this for my son…. And we are *old* parents, so he will have to go through this [loss of a parent] in his 30s rather than in his 50s, as I am doing now."

---

6   *Parenting an Only Child: the Joys and Challenges of Raising Your One and Only*

7   "In Praise of the Ordinary Child," *TIME*, July 23, 2015

Most of the parents I spoke to about not having more than one child cited secondary infertility, limited resources, career concerns, failing marriages, or advancing age. They felt they were able to offer their one child more of their time, resources, and energy. More and more Americans are choosing to have only one child to complete their family. So why, in our culture, is the question of when a couple will have another child asked relentlessly of those with one child by family members and others?

Deirdre Clark, a Portola Valley, California, mother of an only child shares that the most frequent response she gets is that such couples tried to have more children but were unable to do so due to health, money, divorce, or their spouses' desires to have no more than one child. A few of the Clarks' friends who decided to have one child say they enjoy their adult lives and could only manage to fit one child in. Others claim time and complexity, as both parents work. One friend said she loves being able to focus on one child.

"Often when people ask how many children we have I say one, and I quickly add that we tried to have more, but it didn't happen," Clark says. "This stops them from probing further. I am touchy about the subject, which is why I tell them we wanted more. I probably feel that parents of larger families think we are selfish for not having more. We actually believe it is better for children to have siblings.

"[Our daughter] didn't like being an only child when she was young. She would constantly ask us to have another baby. When she was in the fifth grade we had an exchange student live with us for a year. She was 16 at the time, and we loved her like a family member. Our daughter thought of her as her older sister. When she left, our daughter said she didn't want to have another exchange student because 'no one can replace Katie.' By the time our daughter entered middle school, she stopped asking for a sibling. She would come home from friends' homes who had siblings and say, 'I am so glad I don't have a brother or sister.' She said she liked not having to share her room or other possessions. 'I like my peaceful home and brothers and sisters would disrupt it.'

"The advantage of having an only child is that you truly can focus on one child. My husband and I have been able to travel a lot, since one child is easy to bring along. Also, we each got plenty of our own time; we would take turns spending time with our daughter while the other got to pursue his or her hobbies.

"Disadvantages are that the child often thinks the world revolves around them. Also, you have to be careful about spoiling them with material goods. Vacations can be lonely for our daughter, so we frequently bring one of her friends. A sibling adds so much to a one's life, and only children need to bond with friends, cousins and other family members. This was the case with my husband—also an only child. His high school friends were and still are a very big part of his life."

Ellen and Bruce Eanet of Bethany Beach, Delaware, decided not to have another child after their son was born. They wanted a boy, they did not want to deal with sibling rivalry, and they had economic and time constraints. Moreover, sending their child to private school was more affordable, as were other child care costs. They believe the quality of their parenting was better with an only child, as they could devote enough time and energy to their son. "From the very beginning, our message was that he completed our family," Ellen says. "He never asked about having a sibling. He liked being an only child."

"Our immediate family at first did not believe we would only have one child. However, they were quite pleased to spend a lot of time with him. He went on many vacations with his cousins and grandparents. And our son was always able to make friends. He went to sleepaway camps, participated in scouts, and did volunteer work. He was quite comfortable befriending people of all ages. I think being an only made him more mature. And he was an early reader because we had time to work with him. He could self-entertain from a very young age."

Brooklyn resident, John Decker, jokes that he and his wife chose to have one child so that they could "outvote" the offspring in their modern family structure where everyone gets a vote. The Deckers realized that their commitment, style of parenting and finances favored having only one child. He acknowledges subtle societal pressure to have a larger family, but never felt it. He also believes they are somewhat at a "social disadvantage, in terms of bigger nuclear families generating more social activities and interactions with siblings' friends." They enjoy the fact that they are able to remain in their apartment without space issues. In their urban neighborhood, where space is limited, having one child is not unusual, as it had been for his mother, who grew up as a singleton in the deep south.

George and his wife Antonia felt intense family pressure to have more than one child. "She needs a sibling!" their relatives would implore. The Milton, Massachusetts, couple started their family when they were in their 40s. "We are so very happy with one," says George. "We don't dumb down our conversations with our daughter so, as a result, she is very mature for her age. I lament that she doesn't have brothers and sisters to play with. But parenting is a young people's game. We feel blessed with one child."

As with anything else in life, not all are given a choice. Eva Plaza, an attorney in Los Angeles, says that having an only child for her was not a calculated choice. But she was "happy that it didn't happen again for them, since career was always very important to [her]."

Kathryn Bernert of San Diego echoes Plaza's sentiment. Bernert received a breast cancer diagnosis when her daughter was only two years old, which curtailed their hope for other children. She has, however, enjoyed a very successful legal career and a lovely, well-adjusted and well-cared for daughter.

Olivia of Potomac, Maryland, thought she would never be able to have children, due to health issues. Her only child was her "miracle child." Olivia "totally enjoyed having only one child, though I know my daughter always wanted a big family. Instead, her friends became my 'other' children and still are. Our Thanksgiving dinner—held on Wednesday night before Thanksgiving—now consists of 22 people, including one or two of the boyfriends and one husband. There are only four guests my age at the table!"

Sompheap Sem, also of Potomac, laments having started a family later in life. He and his wife "wanted to have three children, but could produce only one." Fertility treatments were unsuccessful. They successfully raised an only child—a daughter—who never wanted for anything materially and was happy, smart and well-adjusted.

Michelle Delino of Chevy Chase, Maryland, also had hoped to have more than one child. Following her divorce, she notes, "It was God's choice for us to have just one and now I understand why!" She views having one child as a good thing in their lives, "although [she believes her son] might have benefited by having a sibling to commiserate with." Delino's son "is accepting of [their] circumstances and has always expressed he's happy to be an only child."

Danny Wolff of Olney, Maryland, said that his wife's uterus ruptured at the birth of their daughter. People frequently comment to him that it is "so much easier" having only one child. He appreciates that it is financially advantageous and that with the multitude of activities his child is involved in, it is less difficult to manage schedules with one child.

Georgia Booth Guhin of Chevy Chase, Maryland, did not choose to have one child. A medical issue and bad timing were the cause. "It has been wonderful for us and I don't miss not having another child," she says. "And there are many advantages to having only one, but I do wish our son had a sibling, especially as we are older and have small families. I think parenting has been simpler, however. It's my feeling that we are closer with our son because we are a family of only three. We were able to devote our weekends to his out-of-town sports events without dividing our time and attention. We may have been more patient with him as he was growing up, as well. The danger has always been that we would focus on him too closely and not allow him to breathe and make mistakes."

Boston, Massachusetts, mom Kathryn McHugh and her husband decided on one child because of her age and attendant pregnancy risk factors. As her son aged, they "sometimes find [them]selves wondering about that second child that [they] didn't have, but still feel very blessed to have one healthy child." McHugh has read about or heard some inappropriate comments relating to family size. "It is odd that people would feel empowered to comment on another person's personal choice. But they do."

Los Angeles judge Eric Taylor has one child. "Instincts and an innate desire to be a father" led him to want to have his child. "Then discontent and later divorce ended the urge." Advantages to having one child for Taylor were that it was more affordable, and he believes it builds closer parental bonds. The disadvantage he cited was that his child had no sibling companionship while growing up. Taylor doesn't know if his daughter wanted siblings. "But she doesn't want any more siblings now."

Of course, as Dr. Newman rightly notes, "A child—with or without siblings—is more likely to be content, if his parents are comfortable and happy with their family size. There is no way to convince an only child or teenager that life without siblings is wonderful unless you can accept one child as your own positive reality no matter what the circumstances or choices that got you there."[8] And there is enough judgment in the world that none of us have to

---

8   https://www.psychologytoday.com/blog/singletons/201211/when-your-child-asks-sibling

carry the burden of worrying about that, especially when it comes to whether one chooses to have one child or none at all. A family size once stigmatized in the United States is now commonplace and considered "normal."

Families Who Adopt

"I didn't choose my family. They chose me."

—Angelina,
Phoenix, Arizona

© Varina and Jay Patel

A conversation I heard between two women has stuck with me through the years. "Your daughter is even more loved than mine. I mean, you picked her!" gushed the woman who birthed a daughter to the other who adopted. This attitude lies in stark contrast to a common insult hurled during my childhood: "You were adopted, and your parents just didn't tell you!" For some reason, being adopted decades ago was untethering, scary to children, and rare by today's standards—a state of affairs no longer present today.

Wayne Warner of Lowell, Vermont, adopted two boys of African-American descent. Warner, a successful white country music artist, calls his fatherhood of Kyle and Keenan his "greatest gig." As far as they knew, Warner and his then wife "could have babies, but once we adopted, these were our kids, as far as we were concerned." His marriage "was a victim of show business," but his sons lived with Warner after the divorce.

Warner grew up in the all-white community where he raised his sons and, fortunately, their family has experienced little racism there. One of his sons was asked, "Are you Michael Jordan's son?" As one of the only black people in their northern Vermont town, they have encountered people who believe that "you have to be on an NBA team or related to an NBA player to be black." Many of the people the family knows only had seen black people on television. In third grade, Kyle was called the N-word by a fifth grader. The school principal wanted to call a meeting to address the situation. Warner asked the principal not to do so but instead to give him the student's name so he could invite him over for pizza. Overall, the Warner children were embraced by the community.

Kyle, now twenty-three years old, is teaching in a school for children with special needs. Keenan is eighteen and is considering a career in music. Warner, with the help of other musicians, like Taylor Swift, made a video for an adoption organization, Ark of Hope for Children, called "God Bless the Children,"[1] which addresses the thousands of foster children in this country who dream of being adopted by loving families. Warner and his sons also produced a song and video called "Painted Hands,"[2] which addresses racism and other societal problems, and features artists from every state.

The Warners' closeness is palpable. They are a family emblematic of the notion that love trumps skin color or other differences.

Transracial adoption was controversial a decade ago, and even forbidden by many agencies. In 1972, the National Association of Black Social Workers issued a statement that took "a vehement stand against the placements of black children in white homes for any reason," calling transracial adoption "unnatural," "artificial," "unnecessary," and proof that African-Americans continued to be assigned to "chattel status." The organization was committed to the position that black children's healthy development depended on

---

1   https://www.youtube.com/watch?v=ajRUEShQUlg

2   http://melodicalhearts.org/painted-hands/

having black parents.[3] However, in the United States, there is a vast shortage of families seeking to adopt children of African-American descent, so the strictures loosened. In 1996, Congress enacted a law forbidding agencies from denying or delaying placement of a child for adoption solely on the basis of race or national origin.[4] The debate has dissipated somewhat, but cultural sensitivity still is considered in interracial adoptions.[5]

Same-sex couples are adopting children with increasing frequency today.[6] Some states, however, have in place legal

3   http://nabsw.org.

4   Hollinger, J.H. and The ABA Center on Children and the Law National Resource Center on Legal and Courts Issues. (1998). *A guide to the Multiethnic Placement Act of 1994 as amended by the Interethnic Provisions of 1996.* Washington, DC: American Bar Association.

5   There now are many books and resources that deal with transracial adoption that did not exist a generation ago, such as Rachel Garlinghouse's *Come Rain or Shine: A White Parent's Guide to Adopting and Parenting Black Children* (CreateSpace Independent Publishing Platform, 2013) and Rhonda Roorda's *In Their Voices: Black Americans on Transracial Adoption* (Columbia University Press, 2015).

6   The Williams Institute estimated almost ten years ago that same-sex couples are raising approximately four percent of all adopted children in the United States. Gary J. Gates, M.V. Lee Badgett, Kate Chambers, Jennifer Macomber, "Adoption

barriers—such as only allowing one parent in a same-sex couple to be acknowledged legally as the parent—that make adoption more difficult for gay couples. One couple I interviewed was counseled by their first adoption agency in Maryland to send only one person to the hospital and to pretend he was straight. The couple moved to a different agency.

Hannah Wald of Alamo, California, was born in Paraguay and raised in New York and California. She was adopted when she was six months old. Her adoptive parents are white Americans of Dutch/Jewish and German/Polish ancestry. Her younger sister was adopted from Guatemala. Before adoption was outlawed in Paraguay, she was lucky to have befriended another adoptee from Paraguay. Wald maintains a sense of pride that she is from a foreign country, which her mother told her at an early age. Her pride is reflected in her "passion for world cultures." Wald was a voracious reader about Paraguay and different countries and cultures, loves to travel and witness these differences firsthand, and has a deep appreciation for the world's diversity. She does, however, admit to having some lingering sadness and confusion about being adopted. "It made me sad to consider the possibility that my birth mother didn't

and Foster Care by Gay and Lesbian Parents in the United States," The Williams Institute, Los Angeles, CA. 2007. With legalization of gay marriage nationwide in 2015, that number is undoubtedly higher today.

want to keep me. I learned that it was because she loved me that she placed me up for adoption. She wanted a better life for me and I thank her very much for that. I love my 'adoptive' parents, but I don't like calling them that. They are my real family, because they gave me the best life possible. They gave me everything that I wanted and needed to have a happy childhood. They loved me unconditionally and I love them unconditionally as well." Wald does wish there had been more diversity in her schools when she was growing up. Her high school was only 5 percent Hispanic. She usually doesn't mind that she doesn't resemble her parents. However, sometimes uncomfortable situations have arisen. "Recently, I was at a baseball game at Wrigley Field and someone asked me where my parents were, even though they were standing with me. Things like that sometimes sting."

Other people I interviewed related stories of difficulties that were encountered where the adopted child did not resemble his or her adoptive parents. For example, Sunni Knowlton of Phoenix, Arizona, was bullied for looking Asian when she was a child in the Midwest, adopted by white parents. She continues to bear those scars today.

Australian diplomat Janette Ryan, who lives in Maryland, resents the "Is she your *real* daughter?" query she receives regarding her adopted Columbian-born daughter. "Yes, she is my real daughter," with no further explanation, is how Ryan responds. She believes that the strong answer comforts her daughter, who is aware of her origins, but appropriately regards Ryan as her mother nonetheless. Ryan acknowledges that, because she is Anglo, she is not among those mistaken as her daughter's nanny. She also knows that if she were the darker-skinned, "that racist assumption would be turned on its head."

Adoptees also related the sting of feeling different. Shareen Pine, of Washington, D.C., was adopted from India to white parents in Massachusetts. She wrote in *The Washington Post Magazine*, "There was no space for me to be confident or beautiful because I was too busy wanting to be white or petite or not-adopted."[7] However, she is now "so grateful that my daughter is growing up in a community where brown can be beautiful."[8]

Elise Stigliano of Silver Spring, Maryland, adopted two children because she was unable to birth children. "Adoption already was an element in my life," says Stigliano. "My sister is adopted, as is my niece.

"Neither of my kids look like us, especially my son. Once, when he was an infant, a five-year-old looked into

---

7   Shaaren Pines, "I Was Adopted and the Pain Lingers," *The Washington Post Magazine*, January 11, 2015.

8   *Id.*

the carriage, then at me and back at my son and yelled as loudly as she could, 'This mom has the wrong baby!' Several times adults would ask, 'Are you really his mother?'

"I know other adoptive parents in my neighborhood and we support each other informally, not in groups. However, I have attended post-adoption meetings at The Barker Foundation, through which we adopted our children and have met more adopting families there.[9]

"The journey brings you to internal places of emotion, knowledge and awareness that you could not imagine going. The idea of 'family' changes and broadens. The idea of global connection enhances, especially if your children are mixed race or look very different from you. You begin to see the 'sameness' barriers break down. It is very freeing and the support system for your whole life also expands."

Arohi Pathak, also of Silver Spring, has wanted to adopt since she was a young adult. "I never felt the need to have my own biological child and I have a partner who has supported that decision one hundred percent.

"In the beginning of the adoption process, my father was skeptical about our decision, cautioning us against it.

---

9   I was a foster parent to one of Stigliano's children when they were awaiting their adoption. People assumed their brown-skinned baby was mine, and not Stigliano's during those early days, based on the colors of our skin.

This probably had more to do with stigma, since he lives in India, where adoption still carries a stigma for the older generations. But since our son has been in his life, there is nothing but acceptance and love on his part.

"We are very careful to make sure our son grows up knowing that adoption is just as normal as any other way to create a family."

Karen Schmelzer Jacobsen, a social worker from Pittsburgh, Pennsylvania, adopted two children. During the first 18 years of her marriage, she was among the 20 percent of women with unexplained infertility. She was open to adoption before her husband was ready. "It takes two to say yes, but only one to say no," Karen quips.

The couple was resistant to open adoption, fearing that birth parents might change their minds about adoption after bonds already were formed with a baby they hoped to adopt. Now she cannot imagine having a closed adoption. Her adopted children were eager to meet their birth parents at a certain point and appreciated the opportunity to have done so.

Karen did not learn that her own mother had been adopted until Karen became an adult. "There was something considered shameful about it in my parents' generation. It was a big secret that no one outside of her immediate family knew. When we wrote our adoption letter [to prospective birth parents], I asked my mother if I could include in the letter the fact that she was adopted. Her story became public, and it was a freeing moment for her after 80 years of secrecy. And my son and daughter like that they have being adopted in common with their grandmother."

At age 45, following two adoptions, Karen was surprised to find herself pregnant with a son, Mark. Her adopted son, Jack, maintained that his prayers for a brother finally were answered. As Mark got older, he lamented that he wanted two sets of parents like his siblings had. "He thinks it is unfair that he doesn't have two sets," Karen laughs.

"Families are built so many different ways," Karen says. She and her husband worked for organizations supporting homeless children and individuals with disabilities. While they were keenly aware of opposing views regarding transracial adoption, they did not allow other people's beliefs to affect their decisions. They followed their hearts and adopted children who are of mixed racial ancestry. Though their neighborhood is not very diverse, Karen has not witnessed any insensitive comments relating to her children's differing ethnicity.

She was, however, offended when she was pregnant and several people referred to her now having a baby of her "own." The irony is that her "two older children were planned. The third was not."

"My children are three miracles. The five of us make our family. We live in a more accepting world than that of my parents' generation, though there is still some boundary crossing and ignorance out there. Each family has their own story, and our family came together in an interesting and beautiful way."

A Word from the Professionals

> "The new normal in modern American families is
> just about anything you want it to be."
>
> —Dr. Anita Gadhia-Smith

Part of my work in examining how much modern American families have changed involved discussions with mental health professionals about what these changes have meant for our society. Most found that the lessened strictures on what constitutes a "normal" family today meant more freedom, less shame and more sharing.

M.R. Kravitz, MA, LPC, practitioner and owner of The Family Center Bethesda in Maryland views these changes with sanguinity:

> "As our species evolves, with extended life spans, with societal, economic, physiological, psychological, vocational, educational, political, environmental, and developmental changes, there come familial changes. Each domain plays a part and has impact. Our concept of family continues to change. We are a brilliant rainbow of temperaments and personalities within one species and within each family. Each family has its own culture. Within each family's culture, there are

often sub-cultures that sometimes are more clearly represented within each generation. However, even a generation has many cultures. Within our American culture is a plethora of cultures and of sub-cultures.

"Having open conversations regarding 'family values' has become more culturally comfortable in today's world, yet it still holds great challenges and obstacles. Strangely enough, psychology is a young science and, therefore, we are still a very young species in developmental terms. With each era, we note psychological and cultural changes, we see changes within family cultural paradigms, and our expectations as and for individuals, as well as for families, continue to change. Being open to and willing to have discussions, without hypothesis or agendas, is evidence of our psychological development."

Simple changes in the way our society operates are catching up to changing familial norms. I notice more forms for schools, medical organization and the government that allow for identifying one's self and family in ways not permitted a generation ago. My daughter attends a university in Chicago and my son in Boston. Both schools presented us with forms that allowed more room for different types of family structures and living situations. And, when I am called upon to fill out forms for various things, more often than not, I can check "other" when it comes to "race." Sometimes even "multicultural" is an option. When I was growing up as a biracial child and young adult, I never knew what box to check. So sometimes I put caucasian and sometimes I chose Asian/Pacific Islander.

Social worker, Kate Olsen, has recognized changes in school paperwork in the New England schools with which she has dealt as well. She and her wife, and others, have worked to get standard forms to say "parent 1" and "parent 2" and have seen that more schools recognize that there might be different addresses due to divorce. She notes that such changes are more welcoming, especially for families new to a school or other organization.

Keeping up with changes in our society can present challenges for those who serve individuals in our evolving family structures. Washington, D.C., clinical psychologist and success coach, Dr. Nicole Cutts observes:

> "Mental health and medical practitioners need to be aware of their biases when serving our diverse American public. For example, heterosexist and heteronormative language in both the patient intake process and treatment can create microagression that the practitioner may be completely unaware of and yet so damaging to patients and clients. For example, many intake forms assume a 'traditional' family structure with words like spouse, husband or wife. Practitioners should examine their own biases and assess their forms and language to be sure they are inclusive of diverse backgrounds. From the patient/client perspective, people should seek out practitioners with which they

feel comfortable and who can honor the diversity in their family structure or life as a single person."

Dr. Anita Gadhia-Smith, psychologist and author in Washington, D.C., has counseled individuals, couples and families for more than 20 years.

"Over the years, I have seen more varying types of families—inter-ethnic, mixed-race, single parents, including women who choose to have children on their own, same-sex parents, and more blended families. There are now more often 'out of the traditional family box' families that I am seeing.

"With these changes, I am seeing a new freedom and openness. There is less secrecy and shame. As the stigmas have decreased in the culture over the last ten to 20 years, I've seen more openness in my patients. There has been a great cultural shift with liberalism in relationships. It is freeing for people to feel more comfortable in whatever family they have chosen to create.

"I also have seen more sexual fluidity—people in hetero relationships that move into homosexual relationships. This change raises new issues. There is more self-acceptance, and more complexity in and redefinition of what constitutes a family. People now are able to self-define many other ways of being a family than what was previously accepted in society. The new normal is that there isn't a new normal anymore. It is what works for each individual. The standard formula of a family only being made up of a husband, wife, and children no longer exists."

Spiritual advisors echo these observations. Jeanne Brumbaugh of Warfordsburg, Pennsylvania, has counseled clients for ten years and has seen much evolution in family structures during that time. Brumbaugh says, "There is no such thing as normal or abnormal when it comes to working with human beings. Each person's journey is unique to them. But, self-love and self-respect are absolutely essential to providing a healthy foundation for self-care. When one stands, firmly rooted in self-love—not narcissism—self-respect and self-care, well-being on all levels is the fruit which is borne."

D.C. Spiritual Director and former Catholic priest Tom Woods,[1] who counsels individuals from all walks of life, adds:

> "The modern American family, more so than any time in this country's history, comes in a wide range of makeups and dynamics. The 'Cleavers' have left the building....
>
> "For me as a counselor and spiritual director, I follow the example that my faith has blessed me

---

1   Thomas Woods, Founder, Spiritual Director, Public Speaker and Interventionist. www.dcspiritualdirector.com.

with, namely the example of Christ. Jesus always met people right where they were, meaning there were no prerequisites in encountering Him and being loved and listened to and shown God's mercy by Him. He taught them about their/our infinite value as a child of God. He showed them they mattered. He gave them an understanding of their true dignity.

"That said, although family dynamics and makeups may have a new look, a person is still a person, and that has never changed. So in my practice I do my best to mirror Christ, no matter what kind of family they are a part of. I have found that when a person truly comes to embrace that they really do matter, that they have a purpose, that they are loved no matter what, it opens up new spiritual paths that they never knew they had access to, or even existed. They begin to see themselves and others in a new light, and that is when the 'miracle' begins to happen. All they need to do is be open to the possibility, and then something much greater than themselves now has the 'permission'— our free will must offer that 'yes'—to show them the person they have been called to be."

As our society becomes more accepting of changing familial norms, we must all adjust our assumptions and the way we serve others. Those in the mental health field see these changes as positive—not a breakdown of our society, but a healthy expansion.

Moving Forward

There is no ideal family. What works for some doesn't work for others. The good news is that varying choices are now widely accepted. While sometimes laws and social services are slow to keep up with such changes, the point is that there is no "normal." Acceptance of differences grows every year in the United States. The shifts have been dramatic, and for that I am grateful and hopeful.

Even as I write, new familial paradigms are being formed and "normalized." On many school campuses, transgender—or at least gender neutral—restrooms have sprung up to accommodate the rising number of transgender folk in our communities. One of our nation's most famous Olympic athletes—Bruce Jenner, now known as Caitlyn Jenner—came out as transgender this year, and has a popular television show and several high-profile magazine covers to her credit. Blended families or step-siblings are no longer unusual, as they were when I was growing up with five step-siblings. Couples are no longer excommunicated by the Catholic church for divorce, as my parents had been in the 1960s. Couples today frequently marry outside of their religions, ethnic or racial groups, and social classes, and the social pressure not to do so has eased significantly. Older men have long been marrying trophy wives, and now "cougar" women are coupling with younger men, producing children with the use of advanced fertility treatments. These people sometimes endure being mistaken for the grandparents of their own children, as my father did for my half-brother, striking fear in my half-brother that his father was so old he was likely to die soon. Unmarried couples who live together no longer warrant comment. Family members "of choice" frequently are not related by blood at all. Family-friendly locales are peopled by all kinds of groupings who may have retreated to less conspicuous places in past generations. Times are changing.

Of course, evidence of the mythologies of racial and ethnic classification remains omnipresent in our culture. There is a tribal-like desire for inclusion. Amidst crumbling racist stereotypes, homophobia and, to a greater extent, transphobia rear their ugly heads.

Perhaps we owe some of our broadening views to the Internet. It is harder for many to stay xenophobic while our mixing pot continues to expand and visibility increases. Education frequently can eradicate prejudice and increase acceptance. And the Internet at least exposes more people to a wider world.

While part of my goal in writing this book was to raise awareness of insensitivities that occur as our common

American family units change, microaggressions take place in my life—and I suspect in many other minority members' lives—on a daily basis. The lack of malicious intent does not always reduce the frustration. And all of those with whom I spoke commiserated over the effect insensitive comments may have on children. Perhaps an easy rule to follow is simply to assume that the child you see is with his or her parent. After all, would you want your four-year-old daughter to hear a stranger ask you if she is your "real" daughter?

This book is just a starting point for discussion—an accessible overview—and not an exhaustive treatment of the typical changes in the modern American family. Let's keep the dialogue going and raise the vibrations on these issues of primary importance to the fabric of our society and primal urge to belong.

Let's promote diversity education in our schools and our families. The mosaic is expanding, and we are all worthy of inclusion, acceptance, and understanding.

About the Author

 Maria Leonard Olsen is a biracial woman whose parents were forbidden by law to marry in their home state of Maryland in the early 1960s. She is the mother of two children, a lawyer, journalist, and author of the children's book *Mommy, Why's Your Skin So Brown?*

Maria graduated from the University of Virginia School of Law, served in the Clinton Administration's Justice Department, fostered newborn babies awaiting adoption, and has been on the boards of Children's National Medical Center BOV, the Catholic Coalition for Special Education, GirlsUp, and the Alzheimer's Association of Greater Washington. She has written for the *Washington Post, Washingtonian, Bethesda Magazine, Parenting, BabyTalk, and Washington for Women*. She lives in Fairhaven, Maryland.

Index

Bibliography / References

Books:

Bennett, Michael Gordon. *7-10 Split: My Journey as America's Whitest Black Kid*, Bennett Global Entertainment, 2015.

Bolick, Kate. Spinster: *Making a Life of One's Own*, Crown, 2015.

Cain, Madelyn. *The Childless Revolution: What It Means To Be Childless Today*, Da Capo Press, 2001.

Casey, Terri. *Pride And Joy: The Lives And Passions Of Women Without Children*, Atria Books, 2007.

Chang, Sharon. *Raising Mixed Race: Multiracial Asian Children in a Post-Racial World*, Routledge, 2015.

Coates, Ta-Nehisi, *Between the World and Me*, Spiegel & Grau, 2015.

Daum, Meghan. *Selfish, Shallow, and Self-Absorbed: Sixteen Writers on the Decision Not to Have Kids*, Picador, 2015.

Defago, Nicki. *Childfree and Loving It!* Vision, 2005.

Durrow, Heidi. *The Girl Who Fell From the Sky*, Algonquin Books, 2011.

Eubanks, W. Ralph. *The House at the End of the Road: The Story of Three Generations of an Interracial Family in the American South*, Smithsonian, 2009.

Garlinghouse, Rachel. *Come Rain or Shine: A White Parent's Guide to Adopting and Parenting Black Children*, CreateSpace Independent Publishing Platform, 2013.

Gates, Gary J. and M.V. Lee Badgett, Kate Chambers, Jennifer Macomber. *Adoption and Foster Care by Gay and Lesbian Parents in the United States*, The Williams Institute, 2007.

Hollinger, J.H. and The ABA Center on Children and the Law National Resource Center on Legal and Courts Issues. *A Guide to the Multiethnic Placement Act of 1994 as amended by the Interethnic Provisions of 1996* American Bar Association, 1998.

Ireland, Mardy. *Reconceiving Women: Separating Motherhood from Female Identity*, Guilford Press 1993.

Jackson-Nakazawa, Donna. *Does Anybody Else Look Like Me?: A Parent's Guide to Raising Multiracial Children*, Da Capo Press, 2004.

Knobler, Claude. *More Love, Less Panic: 7 Lessons I Learned About Life, Love, and Parenting After We Adopted Our Son from Ethiopia*, TarcherPerigee, 2015.

Newman, Leslea. *Heather Has Two Mommies*, Alyson Books, 1989, Candlewick, 2015.

Newman, Susan. *The Case for The Only Child*, HCI, 2011.

Newman, Susan. *Parenting an Only Child: The Joys and Challenges of Raising Your One and Only*, Broadway Books, 2001.

Notkin, Melanie. *Otherhood: Modern Women Finding A New Kind of Happiness*, Seal Press, 2014.

O'Hearn, Claudine Chiawei. *Half and Half: Writers on Growing Up Biracial and Bicultural*, Pantheon, 1998.

Olsen, Maria Leonard. *Mommy, Why's Your Skin So Brown?* Mirror Publishing, 2013.

Rankine, Claudia, and Beth Loffreda, Max King Cap. *The Racial Imaginary: Writers on Race in the Life of the Mind*, Fence Books Science Library, 2015.

Ratliff, Sarah, and Bryony Sutherland. *Being Biracial: Where Our Secret Worlds Collide*, Coquí Press, 2015.

Roorda, Rhonda. *In Their Voices: Black Americans on Transracial Adoption*, Columbia University Press, 2015.

Ruiz, Don Miguel. *The Four Agreements: A Practical Guide to Personal Freedom (A Toltec Wisdom Book)*, Amber-Allen Publishing, 1997.

Scott, Laura. *Two Is Enough: A Couple's Guide to Living Childless by Choice*, Seal Press, 2009.

Souto-Manning, Mariana. *Multicultural Teaching in the Early Childhood Classroom: Approaches, Strategies and Tools, Preschool-2nd Grade*, Teachers College Press, 2013.

Walker, Ellen. *Complete Without Kids: An Insider's Guide to Childfree Living by Choice or by Chance*, Greenleaf Book Group, 2011.

Walters, Kaye. *Kidfree & Lovin' It!–Whether by Choice, Chance or Circumstance: The Complete Guide to Living as a Non-parent*, Serena Bay Publishing, 2012.

Wright, Marguerite. *I'm Chocolate, You're Vanilla: Raising Healthy Black and Biracial Children in a Race-Conscious World*, Jossey-Bass, 2000.

*   *   *

Articles:

Alpert, Emily. "Interracial Couples Increasingly Common, Though Many Aren't Marrying" *Los Angeles Times*, August 31, 2013.

Bever, Lindsey. "Children of Same-Sex Couples Are Happier and Healthier Than Peers, Research Shows" *The Washington Post*, July 7, 2014.

Bolick, Kate. "All the Single Ladies" *The Atlantic*, November, 2011.

Bu, F. "Sibling Configuration, Educational Aspiration and Attainment" *Institute for Social and Economic Research*, 2014.

Combe, Rachel. "At the Pinnacle of Hillary Clinton's Career" *Elle*, April 15, 2012.

Frey, William H. "Multiracial Marriage on the Rise" Brookings.edu, December 18, 2014.

Kluger, Jeffrey. "In Praise of the Ordinary Child," *TIME*, July 23, 2015.

Pines, Shaaren. "I Was Adopted and the Pain Lingers," *The Washington Post Magazine*, January 11, 2015.

Sandler, Lauren. "The Childfree Life: When Having It All Means Not Having Children" *TIME*, August 12, 2013.

Sawhill, Isabel. "20 Years Later, It Turns Out Dan Quayle Was Right About Murphy Brown and Unmarried Moms" *The Washington Post*, May 25, 2012.

Shen, Fern. "Defining Marriage" *The Washington Post*, March 17, 2004.

Sullivan, Paul. "Work-Life Balance Poses Challenges Regardless of Wealth" *New York Times*, October 9, 2015.

*   *   *

Documentaries:

Craft, Lucy, and Karen Kasmauski, Kathryn Tolbert. *Fall Seven Times, Get Up Eight: The Japanese War Brides* Blue Chalk Media, 2015

Frappier, Jennifer. *Chill: A Modern-Day Journey to Motherhood* New York Foundation for the Arts, 2016.

Osborne, Maya. Mark Osborne, dir. *Confessions of a Quadroon*, 2016.

PBS/WETA, *My Journey Home*, 2008-2016.

*   *   *

Web Series:

Harris, Lindsay. *Evoking the Mulatto: Exploring Black Mixed Identity in the 21st Century*, 2012-2016.

Malia, Katie. Chris McPherson, dir. *Almost Asian: Group Therapy*, 2015-2016

* * *

Websites:

Census.gov

ChildlessByChoiceProject.com

EquallyWed.com

FreedomToMarry.org

Gay-family-values.com

HuffingtonPost.com/gay-voices

HuffingtonPost.com/news/childfree

Iglta.org

ImNotTheNanny.com

LGBTQnation.com

MixedRemixed.org

MultiracialMedia.com

MotherInTheMix.com

NPR.org/sections/codeswitch

PewResearch.org

PewSocialTrends.org

Pflag.org

Psychologytoday.com/blog/singletons

SingleMothersByChoice.com

SwirlInc.org

TheChildfreeLife.com

TheLGBTExpo.com

TheMixedExperience.com

TheNotMom.com

VividLife.me

WeAreThe15Percent.com

Yahoo.com/parenting

Youtube.com/watch?v=DWynJkN5HbQ ("What Kind of Asian Are You?, by Helpmefindparents)

CPSIA information can be obtained
at www.ICGtesting.com
Printed in the USA
BVOW11s2335061016

464393BV00007B/12/P

9 781683 190394